PYTHON PROJECTS FOR BEGINNERS

Python at your fingertips! Learn, create, experiment, and don't miss the current programming language. Introduction to data science, coding, and analysis.

ERIC CHAMBERLIN

© Copyright 2020 - All rights reserved.

The content contained within this book may not be reproduced, duplicated or transmitted without direct written permission from the author or the publisher. Under no circumstances will any blame or legal responsibility be held against the publisher, or author, for any damages, reparation, or monetary loss due to the information contained within this book. Either directly or indirectly.

Legal Notice: This book is copyright protected. This book is only for personal use. You cannot amend, distribute, sell, use, quote or paraphrase any part, or the content within this book, without the consent of the author or publisher.

Disclaimer Notice: Please note the information contained within this document is for educational and entertainment purposes only. All effort has been executed to present accurate, up to date, and reliable, complete information. No warranties of any kind are declared or implied. Readers acknowledge that the author is not engaging in the rendering of legal, financial, medical or professional advice. The content within this book has been derived from various sources. Please consult a licensed professional before attempting any techniques outlined in this book.

By reading this document, the reader agrees that under no circumstances is the author responsible for any losses, direct or indirect, which are incurred as a result of the use of information contained within this document, including, but not limited to, — errors, omissions, or inaccuracies.

Table Of Contents

INTRODUCTION 8

CHAPTER 1: PYTHON VERSIONS 10

    PYTHON VERSIONS IMPORTANCE OF CHOOSING AN APPROPRIATE VERSION OF PYTHON 10
    THE DIFFERENCE BETWEEN PYTHON 2 AND 3 11
    HOW DOES PYTHON 2 AND 3 WORK? 16

CHAPTER 2: INSTALLING PYTHON 18

    INSTALLING PYTHON (WINDOWS) 20
    CONNECTING WITH THE PYTHON **SHELL** WINDOW 24

CHAPTER 3: DEFINITIONS: INTERPRETER, TERMINAL, SHELL, AND IDE 28

    SHELL, IDLE, AND SCRIPTS SYNTAX 28
    PROMPT 28
    INDENTATION 29
    INDENTATION PROMPT 31
    PYTHON **SHELL** NAVIGATION 31
    IDLE NAVIGATION 32

CHAPTER 4: VARIABLES AND OPERATORS 34

    PYTHON VARIABLES 34
    OPERATORS 37

CHAPTER 5: DATA TYPES 40

    STRINGS 40
    NUMERIC DATA TYPE 45
    BOOLEANS 46
    LIST 47
    VARIABLES 47

CHAPTER 6: DATA STRUCTURES 62

    SEQUENCE 62
    TUPLES 62
    LISTS 63
    SETS 66
    STRINGS 67

CHAPTER 7: NUMBERS 72

    Working with Numbers 72
    Using Numbers in Python 76
    Addition and Subtraction 76
    Unary Arithmetic Operations 78
    Multiplication and Division 80
    Modulo 81
    Power 82
    Operator Precedence 83
    Assignment Operators 84
    Exercise 2: Multiplying Integers 86

CHAPTER 8: STRING 88

    Accessing Characters in a String 90
    String Indexing 90
    The Len() Function 93
    Slicing Strings 94
    Concatenating Strings 99
    Repeating a String 101
    Using the Str() function 103
    Python String Methods 104

CHAPTER 9: TUPLE 110

    Python Tuples 110

CHAPTER 10: SETS 118

CHAPTER 11: DICTIONARY 126

    Dictionary 126

CHAPTER 12: CONDITIONAL STATEMENTS 130

    Control Statements 132

CHAPTER 13: LOOPS 144

    The While Loop 148
    Break Statement 150
    Continue Statement 151
    Pass Statement 152
    The Loop Repeat Structure 153
    For-loop 153
    Nested loop 158

CHAPTER 14: BASIC OPERATORS OF PYTHON LANGUAGE 162
- ARITHMETIC OPERATORS 162
- COMPARISON OPERATORS 164
- ASSIGNMENT OPERATORS 166
- MEMBERSHIP OPERATORS 168
- IDENTITY OPERATORS 170

CHAPTER 15: FUNCTIONS AND MODULES 174
- WHY ARE USER-DEFINED FUNCTIONS SO IMPORTANT? 175
- OPTIONS FOR FUNCTION ARGUMENTS 177
- WRITING A FUNCTION 179
- PYTHON MODULES 180
- PYTHON PACKAGE 185

CHAPTER 16: PYTHON LIBRARIES 186

CHAPTER 17: OBJECT ORIENTED PROGRAMMING 188
- CLASSES AND OBJECTS 189
- WRITING CLASSES 190
- MAKING AN INSTANCE: OBJECTS 193
- HOW DOES IT WORK? 193
- INHERITANCE 196
- CHILD CLASSES: WRITING ONE 196
- IMPORTING CLASSES 199

CHAPTER 18: DATA ANALYSIS 200
- WHY CHOOSE PYTHON FOR DATA ANALYSIS? 205

CHAPTER 19: MACHINE LEARNING 208
- WHAT IS MACHINE LEARNING? 208
- ADVANTAGES OF MACHINE LEARNING 210
- APPLICATIONS OF MACHINE LEARNING 211

CHAPTER 20: NETWORK SECURITY WITH PYTHON. 216
- COMPONENTS OF A NEURAL NETWORK 216
- BACKPROPAGATION 220
- PROFITING FROM NEURAL NETWORKS 222
- COMPUTERS OVER BRAINS 223
- SPECIFIC MONEY-MAKING DEFINITION 223
- TRAINING THROUGH DATA 224
- RULES CREATED FOR NETWORKS 224
- WORKING THEM FOR MONETARY GAIN 224
- TRADING SYSTEM 225

Investing Through Networks 225
CHAPTER 21: WEB APPLICATIONS **226**
　　How to Work with Django 229
　　User Accounts 231
　　How to Style and Deploy an App 233
CHAPTER 22: PROJECTS **236**
　　Project 1 236
　　Project 2 238
CONCLUSION **244**

Introduction

Python is an incredibly easy computer programming language to learn and is also one of the most useful. Many of today's largest websites are built using Python. Just to show how popular and how powerful it really is, even NASA uses it. It is the best language for any beginner to start computer coding, giving you a great platform from which to move on to bigger and better things.

To help you learn the language, I have included exercises with the chapters and, of course, the answers as well.

The biggest advantage for learners of Python is that you do not have to compile the code. In C++, you have to compile the entire program first and then run it. Only then will you be able to see whether your program runs or returns an error. Python offers the same level of programming, even at a higher stage; but still it is an interpreted language that can be easily written, edited, and corrected.

Given the increasing applications of Python, learning it is extremely profitable from the angle of the global job market. Python can give you the much-needed edge over others when it comes to securing high paid jobs.

The following chapters will discuss all of the different parts of learning how to do some of your coding in the Python language. There are a lot of different reasons why you will want to learn how to work with the Python language, and we want to make sure that we can learn how to make them work for our needs. There are a lot of options out there for learning how to code and get things done with programming, but you will find that the Python language is going to be one of the best ones to work with. This guidebook will show you why that is.

CHAPTER 1:

Chapter 1: Python Versions

Python Versions Importance of choosing an appropriate version of Python

Choosing a correct version of Python can be challenging for both experienced and newcomers. There are few syntactical differences between versions 2 and 3. You can run both versions on the computer and see which works better for you. In case you know one version, then learning the other one is not that difficult.

Most of the programmers learn Python 2 even after they are done with Python 3. This is due to the fact that Python 2 has some interesting aspects from its C language heritage and the way it has been evolved since inception. However, Python 3 is a more consistent programming language; but still most of the frameworks work on Python 2.

Another version, 2.7, has also been widely used due to its packages which include dictionaries such as Pandas, Scikit-learn, NumPy, etc. These can make implementation of machine learning algorithms much easier.

However, experts have advised that if you are just beginning to learn Python, then one should go for version 3.4x, since it has many add-on features along with bug fixes.

One can visit the official Python programming language to learn about all the versions of this language since the beginning.

The Difference Between Python 2 and 3

A common difference between the two versions is the **print** function. Python 2 did not really use a lot of parentheses, i.e. **print ()**. This change may not seem like such a big deal, but it makes all the difference. The print statements in Python 2 have been replaced with **print ()**. When you write a code that you want to print without the parenthesis in Python 2, the code goes on to be readable and is translated. However, if you do this in Python 3, it will report a syntax error. Python 2 does not have much of a problem when it comes to this. The syntax in the two versions differs.

But what is syntax? Syntax is the set of rules used during the coding process.

One other difference is the **integer division**. Python 2 tends to round off the division to the nearest number, while Python 3 tends to be more accurate compared to the version it surpassed. If you are planning on porting Python 3 code into Python 2, you should be careful. A syntax error will not appear if you make a mistake. Hence, you would want to be very careful. For example, instead of using 3/2 in your script, you should consider implementing float 3/2.0 or (3) /2 if you are using Python 3.

Python 2 and Python 3 differ in how they represent their characters. Python 2 can use both ASCII and Unicode strings. Python 3, on the other hand, uses Unicode strings. In ASCII, the byte string is used, which is represented by 'str.' The 'Unicode' implies the Unicode string type. The 'str' and 'Unicode' are subclasses of a common base class. If you want to create a string in Python 2, you can write **str()**. If you want to create Unicode, it is the same: you write **Unicode()**. Python 3 has only one string which is named **str**, which is a Unicode. The sequence of bytes is represented as a byte. There are instances where bytes allows some systems that use ASCII. However, this is not true in all cases.

Python 2 and Python 3 also differ in ranges. Python has two functions which are **range** and **xrange**. One crucial aspect to keep in mind is that range and xrange function the same way, although they are a bit different. The range function was used in Python 3, while xrange was used in Python 2. However, the range function in Python 3 was removed, which gave way to xrange, which is used in Python 2, since it has been found to be faster. So, what is the difference between the range and xrange?

Range and xrange will provide you a way to come up with a list of integers you can use in any way you want to use them. However, xrange will return an xrange object, while range will return a Python list of objects.

Let us get deeper into this! What this means is that range is able to create a static list during runtime, as opposed to xrange, where the values are yielded. Objects known as **generators** are used during yielding. Now, if you want to generate a huge range, let us say over hundreds of millions – the xrange function should be the function that you use. The problem in using range is that if you want to create a huge list like the one stated above, the range function will use up a lot of memory in order to generate your integers. If this happens, your program or software will produce a memory error and it will eventually crash.

Even after xrange from Python 2 was adopted in Python 3, range in Python 3 has a new function. The function is called an underscore in human language (_). This new function is not found in Python 2. This function is said to speed up lookups in the Python 3 version at a dramatic rate, in comparison to the previous range. Instead of using floats, the range uses integers. According to some sources, this function has not yet been added to Python 2. However, the difference is not that much when it comes to the range or xrange in Python 2, since it does not have the underscore (_) function.

There is a difference in speed when it comes to both Python 2 and 3. This is because of both the xrange and the range functions. People who have used the two versions have reported that even though these two versions are implemented in the same way, Python 2 is fast in speed as compared to Python 3.

Now that we have looked at the differences between the two versions of Python, we will briefly go over how to program when it comes to both versions. The first thing you have to do is install the Python interpreter on your computer. This program allows your computer to read Python and carry out its commands. You cannot program if you do not have this program. You will need to get a tutorial that will guide you in the step-by-step process that you will need to undertake. The instructions are mostly the same, but they will differ in some instances, depending on the operating system that you are using.

Now, if you are going to program your software using Python, you will need to begin your own graphical user interface (better known as GUI) for all your codes. The built-in GUI for Python is known as Tkinter – it comes installed in your Python software. After creating a GUI, it is time to make the next move – build your own calculator.

After building your own calculator, you have to create a GUI for your calculator, and then move on to enter the main code. Still, on the main code, you will need to submit a button command. All this may sound new or overwhelming, but this is just a brief description of the programming process while using the Python program. After entering the code, you will need to process the input received from the user, from a string into integers.

The next step is packaging and distribution. Any application which you develop using Python will be in a Python package. However, if you use packaging and distribution, you will be able to make your software independent. Hence, you will be able to install it on any system.

If you want to make your program independent, you will need distribution and packaging tools. The packaging and distribution tools will vary depending on your operating system and the version of Python (Python 2.x or Python 3.x) that you are using. You can use tools such as Python Package Index, Py2exe, Py2app, Pynsist, PyInstaller, and Cx_Freeze, amongst several other tools.

We have looked into a brief procedure that you can use for programming using Python, and also for developing your own software using your Python. It is important to check which packaging and distribution tools are suitable for the version of Python that you are using or for the operating system that you have. For example, Py2app is a freeze tool that is specifically used in the Mac operating system, while Py2exe is a freeze tool that can only be used on the Windows operating system. The tools have different functions.

Pynsist, on the other hand, creates a window installer which installs the version of Python that you specify, hence, installing your application. Pynsist works differently as compared to freezing applications. It does not try to freeze your application into an .exe file. Instead, it makes shortcuts which launch the .py files. Why is this relevant? Well, because of this, certain kind of bugs are avoided.

How Does Python 2 and 3 Work?

It is important to know how Python 2 and Python 3 work. We are going to generally look at how Python works. We had previously mentioned that Python is an interpreted language. We are going to expound on that, and we will see how an interpreter works.

An interpreter is able to translate high-level languages into low-level languages when the program is run. This was previously mentioned: this is just a brief recap of what had been previously discussed. Now, what happens in an interpreter is that you get to write your program in the text editor or a similar program to this. After you do that, you will proceed to instruct the interpreter to run the program. The interpreter goes over each line, one line at a time, and it translates each of them systematically before running it. What are the features of the interpreter program?

One of the features is that the interpreter program spends a small amount of time analyzing and processing the program. One of the reasons the process is fast could be because the interpreter runs from its own source code. After processing and analyzing the code, the resulting code is an intermediate code. What does this mean? What is an intermediate code? An **intermediate code** is a basic structure in which user created and built-in translators are able to operate. The resulting code of an interpreter program is interpreted in another program. The other feature of the interpreter is that program execution is not fast-it is relatively slow.

CHAPTER 2:

Installing Python

Step-by-Step Setup

Start by going to Python's webpage at *www.Python.org* and download Python. Next, we will go through the manual installation, which requires several steps and instructions. It is not obligatory to setup Python manually; however, this gives you great control over the installation, and it is important for future installations that you will perform independently, depending on the specifications of every project. The easier way of installing Python is through automatically installing a scientific data distribution, which sets you up with all the packages and tools you may need (including a lot that you will not need). Therefore, if you wish to go through the simplified installation method, head down to the section about scientific distributions.

When you download Python from the developer's website, make sure to choose the correct installer depending on your operating system. Afterwards, simply run the installer. Python is now installed; however, it is not quite ready for our purposes. We will now have to install various packages. The easiest way to do this is to open the command console, and type **pip** to bring up the package manager. The 'Easy Install' package manager is an alternative, but this is widely considered an improvement. If you run the commands and nothing happens, it means that you need to download and install any of these managers. Just head to their respective websites and go through a basic installation process to get them. But why bother with a package manager as a beginner?

A package manager like pip will make it a lot easier for you to install / uninstall packages or roll them back, if the package version causes some incompatibility issues or errors. Because of this advantage of streamlining the process, most new Python installations come with pip pre-installed. Now let us learn how to install a package. If you chose 'pip', simply type the following line in the command console: pip install < package_name >

If you chose 'Easy Install', the process remains the same. Just type:

easy_install < package_name >

Once the command is given, the specified package will be downloaded and installed, together with any other dependencies they require in order to run. We will go over the most important packages that you will require in a later section. For now, it is enough to understand the basic setup process.

Installing Python (Windows)

Part of getting started with Python is installing it on your Windows. For the first step of the installation, you will need to download the installation package for your preferred version from this link.

Visiting this link, you will be directed to a page. On that page, you will need to choose between the two latest versions for Python 2 and 3: Python 3.5.1 and Python 2.7.11.

Installing Python (Mac)

If you are using a Mac, you can download the installation package from this link.

The progression of learning is getting further into Python Programming Language. In reality, Python is an adaptable, yet powerful, language that can be used from multiple points of view. This just implies Python can be used intelligently when a code or a declaration is to be tried on either a line-by-line premise or when you are investigating its highlights. Incredibly, Python can be used in content mode, most particularly, when you want to decipher a whole document of declarations or application program.

Working with Python requires most extreme caution – particularly when you are drawing in or connecting with it. This caution is valid for each programming language as well. To draw either in or with Python intelligently, the Command Line window or the IDLE Development Environment can be used.

Since you are an apprentice of either programming or using Python, there will shift ventures on how you could connect with and cooperate with Python programming language. Given below are basic highlights of activities for brisk cooperation with Python.

The Command Line Interaction

Associating with the order line is the least difficult approach to work, as a novice, with Python. Python can simply be imagined by seeing how it functions through its reaction to each finished direction entered on the >>> brief. The Command Line probably will not be the most favored commitment with Python; however, throughout the years, it has demonstrated to be the easiest method to investigate how Python functions for learners.

Launching Python Using the Command Line

If you are using macOS, GNU/Linux, and UNIX frameworks, you should run the Terminal tool to get to the command line. Then again, if you are using Windows, you can get to the Python order line by right-clicking on the Start menu and launching Windows PowerShell.

Directions on programming require a contribution of an order. When you need Python to do something for you, you will train it by entering directions that it knows about a similar yield. This is an adjustment in the order may give the ideal yield; be cautious.

With this, Python will make an interpretation of these directions to guidelines your PC or gadget can comprehend and execute.

Let us take a look at certain guides to perceive how Python functions. Note that you can use the print order to print the all-inclusive program.

"Heydays, Savants!"

1. Above all else, open command line in Python.

2. At that point, at the >>> prompt, type the accompanying (do not leave space among print and the section): print("Heydays, Savants!").

3. Now, you should press enter so as to disclose to Python that you are finished with the direction. Promptly, the direction line window will show Heydays, Savants! In the interim, Python has reacted similarly, as it has been told in the composed arrangement that it can relate with. Then again, to perceive how it will react wrongly when you request that it print a similar string using a wrong linguistic structure for the print order, type and enter the direction on the Python order brief

Print("Heydays, Savants!"). The outcome will be: Syntax error: invalid language structure.

This is what get when you use invalid or fragmented explanations. Note that Python is a case-sensitive programming language. So at whatever point you misunderstand the message, it could be that you composed print with a capital letter. Obviously, there is a choice to print direction, you can simply type your announcement inside statements like this: "Primes, Savants!" Note that an announcement is the words you wish to show once the order is given; the words that can fit in are not confined to the model given here, however.

The Most Effective Method To Leave The Python Order Line
To exit from Python, you can type **quit()** or **exit()** commands. Subsequently, hold **Control+Z** and afterward press **Enter**; the Python should exit.

Your commonality with Python Programming ought to get fascinating now; there are still parts to learn, tolerance will satisfy.

The Area of IDLE: Python's Integrated Development Environment (IDE)

A standout amongst the fascinating pieces of Python is the IDLE (Integrated Development and Learning Environment) apparatus. Despite the fact that this specific device is incorporated into Python's establishment bundle, you can download increasingly refined outsider IDEs as well. The IDLE instrument gives you access to an increasingly effective stage, to compose your code and work engagingly with Python. To get to IDLE, you can experience a similar organizer in which you found the direction line symbol or the start menu (as you have gained from order line collaboration). When you click on the IDLE symbol, you will be coordinated to the Python Shell window. This will take us to the segment on cooperation with the Python Shell Window.

Connecting with the Python Shell Window

When you are at the Python Shell Window, you will see a dropdown menu and a >>> prompt, that resembles what you have found in the direction line window (the principal connection talked about). There is a specific IDLE's function of altering for the drawing in past order. Now, you will use a similar IDLE's altering menu to look back to your past directions, and cut, copy, and glue past statements, and taking all things together, make any type of editing. Clearly, the IDLE is increasingly similar to a jump from the direction line association. Incredibly, in the **Menu** dropdown of the Python Shell window are the accompanying menu things: **File, Windows, Help, Shell, Options, Edit,** and **Debug**. Every one of these menus has various functions. The Shell and Debug menus are used while making bigger projects, as they give get highlights to the procedure. In any case, while the Shell menu gives you a chance to restart the Shell and look at the Shell's log for the latest reset, the **Debug** Menu has loads of valuable things for following the source record of an exemption, and featuring the blundering line. With the **Debugger** option, you will most likely introduce an intelligent debugger window that will enable you to step, and look through the running projects on the Python. The **Options** menu of the window enables you to edit and set IDLE to suit your own Python working inclinations.

Moreover, at the **Help** menu, you are opened to choose **Python Help** and other documentation.

Using the **File Window** menu, you will most likely make another document, open a module, open an old record, as well as spare your session through the essential things naturally made once you get to this menu. With the **New File** alternative, you will almost certainly make codes you should simply to tap on it. When you have, you will be taken to another window with a straightforward and standard word processor, where you can type or alter your code. You will see that the record is untitled. Do not freeze as this is the underlying name of the document; it will change when you spare your code. One awesome thing about the menu in the **File** window is that it does not have both the Shell and menu choices together, so the bar changes somewhat in the Shell window. What happens is that in the Shell Window, two new menus have been presented, which are the **Run** and the **Format** menus. At whatever point you need to run the codes you have composed on the record window, the yield will be given in the Shell window individually.

Toward the start of this area, you are informed that Python can be used in the Script Mode. How would you do this? The method of getting the outcome is very extraordinary at this point. When working in content mode, the outcome you will get will not be programmed as in the manner you would in connecting with or associating mode. You should summon them out of your code. To get your yield on this mode, run the content or order it through the print () work inside your code.

To finish up this section, you have been taken through the essential two methods of the Python Programming Language; the drawing in or associating, and the Script modes. Whatever the circumstance, realize that the fundamental change is that one outcome is dependent on order while the other is programmed.

CHAPTER 3:

Definitions: Interpreter, Terminal, Shell and IDE

Shell, IDLE, and Scripts Syntax

Programming languages, just like a regular human languages, such as English, have grammar/writing rules or syntax. Syntax rules in programming languages are simple but strict. Unlike humans, the computer and computer programs, such as compilers and interpreters, cannot understand context. They require precise and proper statements to know what you want. A simple syntax error can either stop your program from functioning or make the computer put a stop to your program. This book will not discuss every syntax rule in this section. It will, instead, teach you one on a need-to-know basis. Syntax rules, after all, are dependent on the things you are writing. And since you do not actually have anything to write yet, this section will introduce you to the basic ones first.

Prompt

The Python Shell and IDLE has a prompt, which looks like this: >>>. You generally start writing your code after the prompt in the Python Shell and IDLE. However, remember that when you write code in a file, a py script, or a module, you do not need to write the prompt.

For example:

Class thisClass():

def function1():

x = 1

print(x)

def function2():

pass

That is valid code.

Indentation

When programming, you will encounter or create code blocks. A **code block** is a piece of Python program text (or statement) that can be executed as a unit, such as a module, a class definition or a function body. They often end with a colon (:).

By default, and by practice, indentation is done with four spaces. You can do away with any number of spaces as long as the code block has a uniform number of spaces before each statement.

For example:

```
def function1():

x = 1

print(x)

def function2():

y = "Sample Text"

print("Nothing to see here.")
```

That is perfectly valid code. You can also use tab, but it is not recommended since it can be confusing, and you will get an error if you mix using tabs and spaces. Also, if you change the **number of spaces** for every line of code, you will get an error. Here is an example in the Shell. Note the large space before print(x)on line 2.

```
>>> x = 1

>>> print(x)

File "<stdin>", line 1

print(x)

^

IndentationError: unexpected indent
```

```
>>> _
```

By the way, a statement is a line of code or instruction.

Indentation Prompt

When using the Python Shell, it will tell you when to indent by using the prompt (...). For example:

```
>>> def function1():
x = 1
print(x)
>>> def function2():
y = "Sample Text"
print("Nothing to see here.")
>>> _
```

In IDLE, indentation will be automatic. Alos, to escape an indentation or code block, you can just press **Enter** or go to the next line.

Python Shell Navigation

You cannot interact using a mouse with the Python Shell. Your mouse will be limited to the window's **Context** menu, including window commands such as **Minimize, Maximize, Close**, and **Scroll**.

Also, you can perform marking (selecting), copying, and pasting, but you need to use the windows **Context** menu for that using the mouse. You can also change the appearance of the window and Shell by going to the **Property** menu.

Most of the navigation you can do in the Shell is moving the navigation caret (the blinking white underscore). You can move it using the navigation keys (left and right arrow keys, PgUp, PgDn, Home, End, etc.). The function of the up and down arrow keys is to browse through the previous lines you have written.

IDLE Navigation

The IDLE window is just like a regular GUI window. It contains a menu bar where you can access most of the functions of IDLE. Also, you can use the mouse directly on IDLE's work area as if you are using a regular word processor.

You might need to take a quick look at the functions of the menu bar for you to familiarize yourself with them. Unlike the Python Shell, IDLE provides a lot more helpful features that can help you with programming.

Primarily, IDLE is the main tool you can use to develop Python programs. However, you are not limited to it. You can use other development environment or word processors to create your scripts.

CHAPTER 4:

Variables and Operators

Python Variables

The Python variables are an important thing to work with as well. A **variable**, in simple terms, is often just going to be a box that we can use to hold onto the values and other things that show up in our code. They will reserve a little bit of the memory of our code, so that we are able to utilize it later on. These are important because they allow us to pull out the values that we would like to use at a later time without issues along the way.

These variables are going to be a good topic to discuss, because they are going to be stored inside of the memory of our code. You will then be able to assign a value over to them and pull them out in the code that you would like to use. These values are going to be stored in some part of the memory of your code and will be ready to use when you need. Depending on the type of data that you will work with, the variable is going to be the part that can tell your compiler the right place to save that information to pull it out easier.

With this in mind, the first thing that we need to take a look at is how to assign a value over to the variable. To get the variable to behave in the manner that you would like, you need to make sure that a minimum of one value is assigned to it. Otherwise, you just save an empty spot in the memory. If the variable is assigned properly to some value, and sometimes more than one value based on the code you are using, then it is going to behave in the proper manner, and when you call up that variable, the right value will show up.

As you go through and work with some of the variables you have, you may find that there are three main options that are able to use. Each of these can be useful, and it is often going to depend on what kind of code you would like to create on the value that you want to put on a particular variable. The three main types of variable that you are able to choose from here will include:

- <u>Float:</u> This would include numbers like 3.14, etc.

- <u>String:</u> This is going to be like a statement where you could write out something like "Thank you for visiting my page!" or another similar phrase.

- <u>Whole number:</u> This would be any of the other numbers that you would use that do not have a decimal point.

When you are working with variables in your code, you need to remember that you do not need to take the time to make a declaration to save up this spot in the memory. This is automatically going to happen once you assign a value over to the variable using the equal sign (=). If you want to check that this is going to happen, just look to see that you added that equal sign is in, and everything is going to work.

Assigning a value over to your variable is pretty easy. Some examples of how you can do this in your code would include the following:

x=12 #this is an example of an integer assignment

pi=3.14 #this is an example of a floating-point assignment

customer name=John Doe #this is an example of a string assignment

There is another option that we are able to work with on this one, and one that we have brought up a few times within this section already. This is where we will assign more than one value to one for our variables. There are a few cases where we are going to write out our code, and then make sure that there are two or more values that go with the exact same variable.

To make this happen, you just need to use the same kind of procedure that we were talking about before. Of course, we need to make sure that each part is attached to the variable with an equal sign. This helps the compiler know ahead of time that these values are all going to be associated to the same variable. So, you would write out something like a=b=c=1 to show the compiler that all of the variables are going to equal one. Or you could do something like 1=b=2 in order to show that there are, in this case, two values that go with one variable.

The thing that you will want to remember when you are working with these variables, is that you have to assign a value in order to make the code work. These variables are also just going to be spots in your code, that are going to reserve some memory for the values of your choice.

Operators

Operators are functions or symbols that indicate a specific operation. For example, the + symbol denotes addition in Mathematics, and is the addition operator in Python. You will recognize many of the operators here as those used in basic Mathematics, but you will also see some that are specific to programming.

The following is a list of the Math operators in Python:

Operation Return

y + z   the sum of y and z added together

y − z   the difference between y and z

-y	the changed sign of y
+y	the identity of y
y * z	the product of y and z multiplied
y / z	the quotient of y divided by z
y // z	the quotient of the floor division of y and z
y % z	the remainder of y / z
y ** z	y to the power of z

CHAPTER 5:

Data Types

Every program has certain data that allows it to function and operate in the way we want. The data can be a text, a number, or any other thing in between. Whether complex or as simple as you like, these data types are the cogs in a machine that allow the rest of the mechanism to connect and work.

Python is a host to a few data types, and, unlike its competitors, it does not deal with an extensive range of things. This is good because we have to worry less and still achieve accurate results, despite the lapse.

Python was created to make our lives as programmers a lot easier.

Strings

In Python, and other programming languages, any text value that we may use, such as names, places, sentences, they are all referred to as **strings**.

A **string** is a collection of characters, not words or letters, which is marked by the use of single or double quotation marks.

To display a string, use the print command, open up a parenthesis, put in a quotation mark, and write anything.

Once done, we generally end with the quotation marks and close the bracket.

Since we are using PyCharm, the IntelliSense detects what we are about to do and delivers the rest for us immediately.

You may have noticed how it jumped to the rescue when you only type in the opening bracket. It will automatically provide you with a closing one.

Similarly, for the quotation marks (single or double), it will provide the closing marks for you.

See why we are using PyCharm?

It greatly helps us out.

Why do we use either single or double quotation marks if both provide the same result?

Ah! Quite the eye.

There is a reason we use these, let me explain by using the example below:

print('I am afraid I will not be able to make it')

print("He said "Why do you care?"")

Try and run this through PyCharm.

Remember, to run, simply click on the green play-like button on the top right side of the interface.

"C:\Users\Programmer\AppData\Local\Programs\Python\Python37-32\Python.exe"
"C:/Users/Programmer/PycharmProjects/PFB/Test1.py"

File "C:/Users/Programmer/PycharmProjects/PFB/Test1.py", line 1

print('I am afraid I will not be able to make it')

^

SyntaxError: invalid syntax

Process is finished with exit code 1

Here is a hint: That is an error!

So, what happened here?

Try and revisit the inputs.

See how we started the first print statement with a single quote?

Immediately, we ended the quote using another quotation mark.

The program only accepted the letter 'I' as a string.

You may have noticed how the color may have changed for every other character from m until won, after which the program detects yet another quotation mark and accepts the rest as another string.

Quite confusing, to be honest.

Similarly, in the second statement, the same thing happened.

The program saw double quotes and understood it as a string, right until the point the second instance of double quotation marks.

That is where it did not bother checking whether it is a sentence or that it may have still been going on. Computers do not understand English; they understand binary communications.

The compiler is what runs when we press the **Run** button.

It compiles our code and interprets the same into a series of ones and zeros, so that the computer may understand what we are asking it to do.

This is exactly why the second it spots the first quotation mark, it considers it as a start of a string, and ends it immediately when it spots a second quotation mark, even if the sentence was carrying onwards.

To overcome this obstacle, we use a mixture of single and double quotes when we know we need to use one of these within the sentence.

Try and replace the opening and closing quotation marks in the first statement with double quotation marks on both ends.

Likewise, change the quotation marks for the second statement to single quotation marks as shown here:

print("I am afraid I will not be able to make it")

print('He said "Why do you care?"')

Now the output should look like this:

I am afraid I will not be able to make it

He said, "Why do you care?"

Lastly, for strings, the naming convention does not apply to the text of the string itself. You can use regular English writing methods and conventions without worries, as long as it is within the quotation marks. Anything outside it will not be a string in the first place, and may or may not work if you change the cases.

Did you know that strings also use triple quotes?

Never heard that before, have you?

We will cover that shortly!

Numeric Data type

Just as the number suggests, Python is able to recognize numbers rather well. The numbers are divided into two parts:

<u>Integer</u> – A positive and/or negative whole numbers that are represented without any decimal points.

<u>Float</u> – A real number that has a decimal point representation.

This means, if you were to use 100 and 100.00, one would be identified as an integer, while the other will be deemed as a float.

So, why do we need to use two various number representations?

If you are designing a program, suppose a small game that has a character's life of 10, you might wish to keep the program in a way that whenever a said character takes a hit, his life reduces by one or two points. However, to make things a little more precise, you may need to use float numbers.

Now, each hit might vary and may take 1.5, 2.1, or 1.8 points away from the life total.

Using floats allows us to use greater precision, especially when calculations are on the cards.

If you are not too troubled about the accuracy, or your programming involves whole numbers only, stick to integers.

Booleans

Ah! The one with the funny name.

Boolean (or bool) is a data type that can only operate on and return two values: true or false.

Booleans are a vital part of any program, except the ones where you may never need them, such as our first program.

These are what allow programs to take various paths if the result is true or false.

Here is a little example: suppose you are traveling to a country you have never been to.

There are two choices you are most likely to face. If it is cold, you will be packing your winter clothes. If it is warm, you will be packing clothes which are appropriate for warm weather.

Simple, right?

That is exactly how the booleans work.

We will look into the coding aspect of it as well.

For now, just remember, when it comes to true and false, you are dealing with a bool value.

List

While this is slightly more advanced for someone at this stage of learning, the **list** is a data type that does what it sounds like.

It lists objects, values, or stores data within square brackets ([]).

Here is what a list would look like:

month=['Jan', 'Feb', 'March', etc.]

We will be looking into this separately, where we will discuss lists, tuples, and dictionaries.

We have briefly discussed these data types.

Surely, they are used within Python, but how?

If you think you can type in the numbers and true and false, all on their own, it will never work.

Variables

You have the passengers, but you do not have a mode of commuting; they will have nowhere to go. These passengers would just be folks standing around, waiting for some kind of transportation to pick them up.

Similarly, data types cannot function alone.

They need to be 'stored' in these vehicles, which can take them places.

These special vehicles, or as we programmers refer to as containers, are called **variables**, and they are the elements that perform the magic for us.

Variables are specialized containers that store a specific value in them and can then be accessed, called, modified, or even removed when the need arises.

Every variable that you may create will hold a specific type of data in them.

You cannot add more than one type of data within a variable.

In other programming languages, you will find that in order to create a variable, you need to use the keyword 'var' followed by '=', and then the value.

In Python, it is a lot easier, as shown below:

name = "John"

age = 33

weight = 131.50

is_married = True

In the above, we have created a variable named 'name' and given it a value of characters.

If you recall strings, we have used double quotation marks to let the program know that this is a string.

We then created a variable called age.

Here, we simply wrote 33, which is an integer as there are no decimal figures following that.

You do not need to use quotation marks here at all.

Next, we created a variable 'weight' and assigned it a float value.

Finally, we created a variable called 'is_married' and assigned it a 'True' bool value.

If you were to change the 'T' to 't', the system will not recognize it as a bool and will end up giving an error.

Focus on how we used the naming convention for the last variable.

We will be ensuring that our variables follow the same naming convention.

You can even create blank variables if you feel like you may need these at a later point in time, or wish to initiate them at no value at the start of the application.

For variables with numeric values, you can create a variable with a name of your choice, and assign it a value of zero.

Alternatively, you can create an empty string as well by using opening and closing quotation marks only.

empty_variable1 = 0

empty_variable2 = ""

You do not have to necessarily name them like this, you can come up with more meaningful names, so that you and any other programmer, who may read your code, would understand.

I have given them these names to ensure anyone can immediately understand their purpose.

Now we have learned how to create variables, let us learn how to **call** them.

What is the point of having these variables if we are never going to use them, right?

Let us create a new set of variables.

Have a look here:

name = "James"

age = 43

height_in_cm = 163

occupation = "Programmer"

I do encourage you to use your own values, and play around with variables if you like.

In order for us to call the name variable, we simply need to type the name of the variable.

In order to print that to the console, we will do this:

print(name)

Output:

James

The same goes for the age, the height variable, and occupation.

But what if we wanted to print them together and not separately?

Try running the code below and see what happens:

print(name age height_in_cm occupation)

Surprised? Did you end up with this?

Print(name age height_in_cm occupation)

^

SyntaxError: invalid syntax

Process finished with exit code 1

Here is why that happened: when you were using a single variable, the program knew what variable that was. The minute you added a second, a third, and a fourth variable, it tried to look for something that was written in that manner.

Since there was not any, it returned with an error that for all practical purposes says, "Umm… are you sure, sir? I tried looking everywhere, but I could not find this 'name age height_in_cm occupation' element anywhere."

All you need to do is add a comma to act as a separator, like so:

print(name, age, height_in_cm, occupation)

Output:

James 43 163 Programmer

Now it says, "Your variables, sir!" It knew what we were talking about. The system recalled these variables and was successfully able to show us what their values were.

But what happens if you try to add two strings together?

What if you wish to merge two separate strings, and create a third-string as a result?

first_name = "John"

last_name = "Wick"

To join these two strings into one, we can use the '+' sign.

The resulting string will now be called a **string object**, and since this is Python we are dealing with, everything within this language is considered as an object, (referring to the object-oriented programming nature of Python we discussed in the beginning).

first_name = "John"

last_name = "Wick"

first_name + last_name

Here, we did not ask the program to print the two strings.

If you wish to print these two instead, simply add the print function and type in the string variables with a + sign in the middle, within parentheses.

Sounds good, but the result will not be quite what you expect:

first_name = "John"

last_name = "Wick"

print(first_name + last_name)

Output:

JohnWick

Hmm. Why do you think that happened?

Certainly, we did use a space between the two variables.

The problem is that the two strings have combined together, quite literally here, and we did not provide a white space (blank space) after John or before Wick; it will not include that.

Even the white space can be a part of a string.

To test it out, add one character of space within the first line of code by tapping on the friendly spacebar after John.

Now, try running the same command again, and you should see John Wick, as a result.

The process of merging two strings is called **concatenation**.

While you can concatenate as many strings as you like, you cannot concatenate a string and an integer together.

If you really need to do that, you will need to use another technique to convert the integer into a string first, and then concatenate the same.

To convert an integer, we use the **str()** function.

text1 = "Zero is equal to "

text2 = 0

print(text1 + str(text2))

Output:

Zero is equal to 0

Python reads the codes in a line-by-line method. First, it will read the first line, then the second, then third, and so on. This means we can do a few things beforehand, to save some time for ourselves.

text1 = "Zero is still equal to "

text2 = str(0)

print(text1 + text2)

Output:

Zero is still equal to 0

You may wish to remember this, as we will be visiting the conversion of values into strings a lot sooner than you might expect.

There is one more way through which you can print out both string variables and numeric variables, all at the same time, without the need for '+' signs or conversion. This way is called **string formatting**.

To create a formatted string, we follow a simple process as shown here:

print(f" This is where {var 1} will be. Then {var 2}, then {var 3} and so on")

Var 1, 2, and 3 are variables.

You can have as many as you like here.

Notice the importance of the white space.

Try not to use the space bar as much.

You might struggle at the start, but will eventually get the hang of it.

When we start the string, we place the character f, to let Python know that this is a formatted string.

Here, the curly brackets are performing the part of placeholders.

Within these curly brackets, you can recall your variables.

One set of curly brackets will be a placeholder for each variable that you would like to call upon.

To put this in practical terms, let us look at an example:

show = "GOT"

name1 = "Daenerys"

name2 = "Jon"

name3 = "Tyrion"

seasons = 8

print(f"The show called {show} had characters like {name1}, {name2} and {name3} in all {seasons} seasons. ")

Output:

The show called GOT had characters like Daenerys, Jon, and Tyrion in all 8 seasons.

While there are other variations to convert integers into strings and concatenate strings together, it is best to learn those variations which are used throughout the industry as standard.

I believe you are in a good position now to begin using those.

Have a look at this result, and keep in mind that I did not use any variable here at all.

Now, you have seen how to create a variable. Recall it, and concatenate the same.

Everything sounds perfect, except for one thing; These are predefined values.

What if we need an input directly from the end user?

How can we possibly know that?

Even if we do, where do we store them?

User-Input Values

Suppose we are trying to create an online form.

This form will contain simple questions like asking for the user's name, age, city, email address, etc.

There must be some way by which we can allow users to input these values on his/her own, and for us to get those back.

We can use the same to print out a message that thanks to the users for using the form and that they will be contacted on their email address for further steps.

To do that, we will use the **input()** function.

The input function can accept any kind of input.

In order to use this function, we will need to provide it with a reference, so that the end user is able to know what he/she is about to fill out.

Let us look at a typical example, and see how such a form can be created:

print("Hello and welcome to my interactive tutorial.")

name = input("Your Name: ")

age = int(input("Your age: "))

city = input("Where do you live? ")

email = input("Please enter your email address: ")

print(f"Thank you very much {name}, you will be contacted at {email}.")

Output:

Hello and welcome to my interactive tutorial.

Your Name: **Sam**

Your age: **28**

Where do you live? **London**

Please enter your email address: **sam@something.com**

Thank you very much, Sam, you will be contacted at sam@something.com.

In the above, we began by printing a greeting to the user, and welcoming them to the tutorial.

Next, we created a variable named 'name,' and assigned it a value that our user will provide us.

In the age, you may have noticed I changed the input to **int()**, just as we changed the integer to string earlier on.

This is because our message within the input parameters is a string value by default, as it is within quotation marks.

You will always need to ensure you know what type of value you are after, and do the needful, as shown above.

Next, we asked for the name of the city and the email address.

Now, using a formatted string, we printed out our final message.

but, how can we print out something we have yet to receive or know?

To answer, I did mention that Python works line by line.

The program will start with a greeting, as shown in the output.

Then, it will move to the next line, and realize that it must wait for the user to input something and hit enter.

This is why the input value has been highlighted by a bold font style here.

The program then moves to the next line, and waits yet again for the user to put something in and press enter. This goes on until the final input command is sorted.

Now the program has the values stored, it immediately recalls these values, and prints them out for the viewer to see in the end.

The result was rather pleasing as it gave a personalized message to the user, and we received the information we need.

Everybody walks away, happy.

Storing information directly from the user is essential and, at times, necessary.

Imagine a game that is based on Python.

The game is rather simple, where a ball will jump when you tap the screen.

The problem is, your screen is not responding to the touch at all for some reason.

While that happens, the program will either keep the ball running, until an input is detected, or it will just not work at all.

We also use input functions to gather information, such as login ID and passwords, to match with the database, but that is a point that we shall discuss later when we will talk about statements.

It is a little more complicated than it sounds at the moment, but once you understand how to use statements, you will be one step closer to becoming a programmer than before.

CHAPTER 6:

Data Structures

Sequence

Sequence is a very basic term in Python that is used to denote an ordered set of values. There are many sequence data types in Python: str, unicode, list, tuple, buffer and xrange.

Tuples

A **tuple** consists of a number of values separated by commas. Tuples are also a sequence data type in Python, like strings and lists. We need to keep in mind that tuples are immutable. It means that they cannot be changed.

The tuples consist of the number of values separated by a comma. The tuples are enclosed in parentheses, while the lists are enclosed in brackets.

Now let us see an example:

>>> m = (14, 34, 56)

>>> m

(14, 34, 56)

```
>>> m[0]
```

14

```
>>> m[ 0:2 ]
```

(14, 34)

Tuples also have the properties like indexing and slicing. Tuples can be nested. Elements in a tuple can be grouped with (). Now let us see an example:

i = 1

j = 2

t1 = i, j # is a tuple consists to elements i and j

t2 = (3, 4, 5) # is a tuple consists to elements 3,4 and 5

t3 = 0, t1, t2 # is a tuple consists to elements 0, t1 and t2

print t3 # result is (0, (1, 2), (3, 4, 5))

Lists

A **list** consists of a number of heterogeneous values separated by commas enclosed by [and], starting from index 0. Lists can be used to group together other values. Unlike Tuples, Lists are mutable in nature. In other words, they can be changed by removing or reassigning existing values. Also, new elements can be inserted to the existing ones.

Now let us see an example:

```
>>> a = [1, 2, 3, 4, 5]
>>> a
[1, 2, 3, 4, 5]
```

As strings, lists can also be indexed and sliced.

```
>>> a = [1, 2, 3, 4, 5]
>>> a
[1, 2, 3, 4, 5]
>>> a[0]
1
>>> a[4]
5
>>> a[ 0:2 ]
[1, 2]
>>> a[ 3:5 ]
[4, 5]
```

Unlike strings, lists are mutable (i.e. the values can be changed)

```
>>> b = [1, 2, 4, 7, 9]
```

```
>>> b
[1, 2, 4, 7, 9]
>>> b[2] = 6
>>> b
[1, 2, 6, 7, 9]
```
Here the index [2] is changed to 6 (the initial value is 4)

```
>>> b[0] = 9
>>> b
[9, 2, 6, 7, 9]
```
{Here the index [0] is changed to 9 (the initial value is 1)}

The values in the list can be separated by using comma (,) between the square bracket. Lists can be nested. List can be used as a **stack** or a **queue**.

For example:

list1 = [1, 2, 3, 4]

print len (list1) # returns 4 - which is the length of the list

list1[2] # returns 3 - which is third element in the list Starts

list1[-1] # returns 4 - which is extreme last element in the list

list1[-2] # returns 3 - which is extreme last but one element

```
list1[ 0:2 ] = [ 11, 22] # replacing first two elements 1 and 2 with 11 and 22

stackList = [ 1, 2, 3, 4]

stackList.append(5)# inserting 5 from the last in the stack

print stackList# result is: [1, 2, 3, 4, 5]

stackList.pop()# removing 5 from the stack Last In First Out

print stackList# result is: [1, 2, 3, 4]

queueList = [ 1, 2, 3, 4]

queueList.append(5)# inserting 5 from the last in the queue

print queueList# result is: [1, 2, 3, 4, 5]

del(queueList[0] )# removing 1 from the queue First In First Out

print queueList# result is: [2, 3, 4, 5]
```

Sets

A **set** does not have any duplicate elements present in it, and it is an unordered collection type. It means it will have all distinct elements in it with no repetition.

Now let us see an example:

```
fruits = ['apple', 'orange', 'apple', 'pear', 'orange', 'banana']
```

basket = set (fruits) # removed the duplicate element apple

print 'orange' in basket # checking orange in basket, result is True

print 'pineapple' in basket # checking pine apple in basket, result is False

a = set('aioeueoiaeaeiou') # create a set without duplicates

b = set('bcokcbzo') # create a set without duplicates

print a # a = ['a', 'i', 'e', 'u', 'o']

print b # b = ['z', 'c', 'b', 'k', 'o']

print a & b # letters in both a and b (A ∩ B) print a | b # letters in either a or b (A □ B)

print a - b # letters in a but not in b (A – B)

Strings

In Python, a **string** is identified by the characters in single quotes (' ') and double quotes (" "). They can only store character values and are a primitive datatype. Please note that strings are altogether different from integers or numbers. Therefore, if you declare a string "111," then it has no relation with the number 111.

>>> print "hello"

hello

```
>>> print 'good'
good
```

The string index starts from 0 in Python.

```
>>> word = 'hello'
>>> word[0]
'h'
>>> word[2]
'l'
```

Indices may also be negative numbers, so start counting from the right. Please note that negative indices start from -1, while positive indices start from 0 (since -0 is same as 0).

```
>>> word = 'good'
>>> word[-1]
'd'
>>> word[-2]
'o'
```

The slicing in Python is used to obtain substrings, while the index allows us to obtain a single character.

```
>>> word = 'develop'
```

```
>>> word[ 0:2 ]
```

'de'

```
>>> word[ 2:4 ]
```

've'

Please note that the starting position is always included the ending position, and is always excluded.

D e v e l o p

0 1 2 3 4 5 6 ---- Index value

In the above example, the word is assigned a value 'develop'. Considering the first statement word, [0:2], the output is de. Here the starting position, d, (0th index) is included, and the ending position, v, (2nd index) is excluded. Similarly, in the second statement word, [2:4], the starting position, v, (2nd index) is included and the ending position, l, (4th index) is excluded.

The important point to be noted in strings is that Python strings are immutable (i.e. strings cannot be changed).

There are many in-built functions available in a string. They are used for various purposes. Let us see some of the basic ones that are most commonly used.

Len: It is the length function that is used to calculate the number of characters present in the string.

Lower: It will convert all the uppercase characters present in the string to lowercase letters. Therefore, after using this function, all characters in the string will be small case only.

Upper: It will convert all the lowercase characters present in the string to uppercase letters. Therefore, after using this function, all characters in the string will be upper case only.

Split: It helps to split the string in parts by using a delimiter. It can be separated using spaces, new lines, commas, or tabs.

CHAPTER 7:

Numbers

Working with Numbers

This data type is used to define and uses any numeric value, either integers or floating-point numbers. Any common mathematical operations such as +, -, *, / can be used on numerical objects. For example, see below.

Integer

>>>5 + 6

11

>>> 88+12

100

>>> 25*4

100

>>> 100**2

10000

Floating Point Number

>>>1.5 + 1.5

3

>>> 2.6+2.4

5.0

>>> 1.5*4

6.0

>>> 5.5/5.5

1.0

Python supports four different numeric data types:

Int: It holds regular integers - 1

Float: It holds floating-point numbers – 1.5

Long: It stores long integers – 123458945L

Complex: It stores complex numbers of the format x+yj. For example, 2+3j, where 2 is the real number and 3 is the imaginary number.

Note that the data type does not need to explicitly be mentioned when declaring variables. Python implicitly understands the amount of memory required for a variable based on the value assigned. Several common arithmetic operations can be done on the numeric value, and they can quickly be tested on the terminal by launching the interpreter, making the Python interpreter act as a calculator.

For example, in the Python Interpreter, you can easily test these operations:

Addition +

Subtraction −

Multiplication *

Division /

Apart from using operators, the programmer can import various packages/libraries, which contain predefined functions that can be applied on data type in order to obtain a required output. For example:

>>>import math

>>>math.sqrt(36)

6

The above statement imports math library using several operations like **sum()**, **sqrt()**, **ceil()**, **floor()**, **factorial()**, **pow()**, **log()** etc.

>>> math.ceil(1.67)

2.0

>>> math.floor(1.67)

1.0

>>> math.pow(6,2)

36

The library includes several functions for trigonometric calculations such **as sin(), cos(), tan(), radian(), and angle()**.

To really understand how useful and fundamental these are, let us look at a real-life example.

Example: A program to calculate simple interest

P=100

N=2

R=3

SI=(p*n*r)/100

print SI

Output: 6

Using Numbers in Python

Numbers are very common in computer programming, and are used as representations of things like money, geographical locations, colors, dimensions, etc. One of the most important of all skills in programming is being able to do mathematical operations effectively, because you will be working with numbers very frequently. Although it helps to have a basic understanding of Math, it is not vital, because you can consider Math to be a tool that helps you to accomplish what you are looking to achieve, and to improve logical thought processes. To start, we will be looking at the two most commonly used number data types in Python – floats, and integers.

A **float** is a number that contains a decimal point, i.e. 3.2, or -0.95

An **integer** is a whole number that may be negative or positive, or it may be zero, i.e. -5, 0, 5

We are going to look at the operators that are used with Python numeric data types.

Addition and Subtraction

Subtraction and addition operators work the same way in Python as they do in Math. You can even use Python as a calculator if you want to. Look at the following examples, beginning with using integers: print(2 + 6)

The output of this is: 8

Rather than passing an integer to print statement directly, we could initialize a variable that stands for the value of the integer: a = 95

b = 125

print(a + b)

The output will be:

220

Do not forget, integers may be a positive number, a negative number or zero, and because of that, we can add a negative and a positive number together: c = -22

d = 51

print(c + d)

The output will be:

29

Addition works in much the same way with float numbers:

e = 8.5

f = 3.5

print(e + f)

The output will be: 12.0

Note that because two float numbers were added together, the returned value is also a float with the decimal place in it

When you use subtraction, the syntax is exactly the same, with the exception of the addition operator being substituted with the subtraction operator: g = 85.95

h = 25

print(g - h)

The output will be: 60.95

In this example, we subtracted the value of an integer from the value of a float, and if there is at least one float in the equation, Python will return the answer as a float.

Unary Arithmetic Operations

These have just one element/component in them and, in the Python language, we can use the addition or subtraction operator as that element together with a value to return the identity of the value (+) or to change the value sign (-). To be fair, this is not a common practive anymore, but you can use + to show the value identity and with a positive value: i = 3.5

print(+i)

The output would be: 3.5

If you use + with a negative value, you will also get the value identity returned, but as a negative value:

j = -25

print(+j)

The output would be: -25

On the other hand, the subtraction operator can also change the value sign. So, if you passed a positive value, the subtraction sign in front of the value returns a value that is negative: i = 3.2

print(-i)

The output would be: -3.2

If on the other hand, you used the subtraction unary operator with a minus value, you would get a positive value returned:

j = -18

print(-j)

The output would be: 18

Unary operations, indicated by the minus or plus signs, return the opposite of the value sign either when – is used or when the identity of the value when + is used.

Multiplication and Division

Similar to subtraction and addition, division and multiplication look the same as they do when used in Math. For multiplication, we use * and for the division we use /. The following example shows a multiplication with two values, both of which are floats: k = 25.1

l = 25.1

print(k * l)

The output will be: 3140.01

When you use division in Python, the quotient is always returned as a float value, regardless of whether you use a pair of integers: m = 55

n = 5

print(m / n)

The output would be: 11.0

This is a big difference between Python 2 to Python 3. Python 3 takes the approach to provide an answer that is fractional, so when / is used to divide 13/2, the output will be 6.5. In Python 2, the answer would be returned as an integer of 6.

The operator in Python 2 can be used to perform floor division, and the quotient x would be returned as the biggest integer number that is equal to or less than x. If you were to run the example above, 555, in Python 2, the output would be 11, with no decimal place.

You can also use to perform floor division in Python 3. If you were to use the expression, 100 / 40, the value returned will be 2. Floor division is very useful when you want the quotient to be returned in a whole number.

Modulo

In Python, we use the % as the **modulo**. This will return the remainder of a division equation rather than the quotient, and is very useful when you want a number that is a multiple of the same number. Let us look at an example: o = 85

p = 15

print(o % p)

The output would be: 10

Broken down, 85/5 will return a quotient of 5, because 15 goes into 85 five times, with 10 left over, so the remainder is 10.

If we were to use floats with the modulo operator, the return value would be a float:

q = 36.0

r = 6.0

print(o % p)

The output would be:

0.0

In this case, 6.0 goes into 36.0 exactly 6 times s there is no remainder, hence the returned value is 0.0.

Power

In Python, we use the ** operator to raise the value on the left to the exponent power on the right. For example, 5 ** 3 – 5 is raised to the 3rd power. In Math, you will normally see this indicated as 5^3. What is going on here is that 5 has been multiplied by itself 3 times. In Python, the same result would be returned whether you ran 5 ** 3, or 5 5 5.

Let us use this with variables:

s = 52.25

t = 7

print(s ** t)

The output would be:

1063173305051.292

When you raise a float number like 52.25 to the power of 7, a large float value will be returned.

Operator Precedence

Remember the order of operations in Math? The same applies in Python arithmetic; operators are evaluated in a specific order, not necessarily from right to left, or left to right. Look at the following: u = 12 + 12 * 6

You can certainly read it from the left to the right, but multiplication will always be done first, so the output would be: 84. The reason for this is that 12 * 6 returns 72. Add the 12 to it and you get 84. If you wanted to do it differently, i.e. add 12 and 12 together, and then run the multiplication. You would need to use parentheses: u = (12 + 12) * 6

print(u)

The output would be: 144

A very easy way to keep precedence order in your mind is through the mnemonic, PEMDAS.

P - Parentheses

E - Exponent

M - Multiplication

D - Division

A - Addition

S - Subtraction

Assignment Operators

You have already used the common one – the equal sign (=). This assignment operator will assign a value from the right, to a variable that is on the left. For example, d = 52 will assign a value of 52 (an integer) to the variable, d.

In computer programming, we mostly use compound assignment operators. These will perform operations on the value of a variable, and will then assign the value, that results from that operation, to the variable. Compound operators are a combination of the equals operator with an arithmetic one; so, if you wanted addition, you would combine + and = to get +=, the compound operator. The following example shows you what that will look like: v = 6

v += 2

print(v)

The output would be: 8

What we did here was set the variable, v as equal to 6. We then used += to add the number on the right of the variable to the left one, and assign v with the result.

We use these operators a lot in loops when you want—a process repeated multiple times. For x in range (0, 7):

x *= 2

print(x)

The output would be:

0

2

4

6

8

10

12

By using the **for-loop** (more about those later), we could automate the += process by multiplying the variable, wby, by 2, and assigning the resulting value in the variable, w, for the next go around of the for-loop.

Python contains one compound assignment operator for each Math (arithmetic) operator that we already covered:

x += 2 #add and then assign the value

x -= 2 #subtract and then assign the value

x *= 2 # multiply and then assign the value

x /= 3 # divide and then assign the value

x //= 5   # floor divide and then assign the value

x **= 2   # increase to the specified power of and then assign the value

x %= 3   # return the remainder then assign the value

These operators are useful when you need to incrementally increase or decrease something, or when you need to automate a process.

Exercise 2: Multiplying Integers

Write a program that will multiply two integer numbers without the use of the * operator

CHAPTER 8:

String

A **string** is an ordered series of Unicode characters which may be a combination of one or more letters, numbers, and special characters. It is an immutable data type, which means that once it is created, you can no longer change it.

To create a string, you must enclose it in either single or double quotes, and assign it to a variable. For example:

\>>>string_one = 'a string inside single quotes'

\>>>string_double = "a string enclosed in double quotes"

When you enclose a string, containing either a single quote or an apostrophe inside single quotes, you will have to escape the single quote or apostrophe by placing a backslash (\) before it.

For example, to create the string, 'I do not see a single quote':

\>>> string_single = 'I do not see a single quote.'

\>>>

When you use the print function to print string_single, your output should be:

>>>print(string_single)

I do not see a single quote.

>>>

Similarly, you will have to escape a double quote with a backslash (\) when the string is enclosed in double quotes.

Hence, to create the string = "He said: "You have been nominated as honorary president of the Mouse Clickers Club."":

>>>string_two = "He said: \"You have been nominated as honorary president of the Mouse Clickers Club. \""

>>>

>>>print(string_two)

He said: "You have been nominated as honorary president of the Mouse Clickers Club. "

>>>

Likewise, a backslash within a string should be escaped with another backlash.

>>> string_wow = "This is how you can escape a backlash \\."

>>>print(string_wow)

This is how you can escape a backlash \.

>>>

Accessing Characters in a String

You can access individual characters in a string through indexing, and a range of characters by slicing.

String Indexing

The initial character in a string takes zero as its index number, and the succeeding characters take 1, 2, 3, etc. as index numbers.

To access the string backwards, the last character takes -1 as its index.

A space is also considered a character.

To illustrate indexing in strings, name a variable 'string_var,' and assign the string 'Python String' with the statement:

>>>string_var = "Python String"

| Index # | 0 | 1 | 2 | 3 | 4 | 5 | 6 | 7 | 8 | 9 | 10 | 11 | 12 |

String	P	y	t	h	o	n		S	t	r	i	n	g
Index	-13	-12	-11	-10	-9	-8	-7	-6	-5	-4	-3	-2	-1
#													

Example #1

To access the first character on the variable 'string_var' (the first character of Python String is P), enter the variable name 'string_var,' and enclose the integer zero (0) inside either the index operator or square brackets [].

>>> string_var[0]

'P'

>>>

In this example, the first character of the string 'Python String' is 'P'. Since the first character takes zero as its index number, Python gives you the letter 'P' as an answer.

Example #2

To access the character on index 8, simply enclose 8 inside the square brackets:

```
>>> string_var[8]

't'

>>>
```

Since 't' takes 8 as it is index number, Python gives you the letter 't' as an answer.

Example #3

To access the character on index 6, an empty space:

```
>>> string_var[6]

' '

>>>
```

Since an empty space takes 6 as it is index number, Python gives you a space (' ') as an answer.

Example # 4

To access the last character of the string, you can use negative indexing in which the last character takes the -1 index.

```
>>>string_var[-1]

'g'

>>>
```

As a string is an ordered list, you can expect that the penultimate letter takes the -2 index, and so on.

Hence, -5 index is:

>>> string_var[-5]

't'

>>>

The Len() Function

There is a more sophisticated way of accessing the last character, and it will prove more useful when you are writing more complicated programs. This is the **len()** function.

The **len()** function is used to determine the size of a string, that is, the number of characters in a string.

For example, to get the size of the variable 'string_var', you will use the syntax:

>>>len(string_var)

13

>>>

By using the **len()** function, Python is able to calculate the number of characters in your string 'Python String.' Do not forget that Python calculates a space as a character. Thus, you get 13 characters.

Since the last character in the string takes an index which is one less than the size of the string, you can access the last character by subtracting 1 from the output of the **len()** function.

To illustrate, type the following on the command prompt:

>>> string_var[len(string_var)-1]

'g'

>>>

Some important notes about accessing strings through indexing:

- Always use an integer to access a character to avoid getting a **Type Error.**

- Attempting to access a character which is out of index range will result in an **Index Error.**

Slicing Strings

You can access a range of characters in a string, or create substrings using the range slice [:] operator. To do this interactively on a random string, simply type the string within single or double quotes, and indicate two indices within square brackets. A colon is used to separate the two indices. The slice operator will give you a string starting with S[A] and ending with S[B-1].

The syntax is: S[A:B-1]

S: The string you wish to use

A: The starting character of the substring you want to create

B: The ending character of the substring you want to create

Example #1

\>\>\>"String Slicer "[2:12]

'ring Slice'

\>\>\>

Index #	0	1	2	3	4	5	6	7	8	9	10	11	12
String	S	t	r	i	n	g		S	l	i	c	e	r
Index #	-13	-12	-11	-10	-9	-8	-7	-6	-5	-4	-3	-2	-1

In this example, we want to create a substring using the range of characters from 'r' to 'e.'

Let us use the syntax S[A:B-1] to understand this command.

S: refers to the string "String Slicer."

A: 2 is the index number which is associated with the letter 'r.'

B-1: 12-1= 11 is the index number which is associated with the letter 'e.'

Therefore, the command says that we are looking for a substring which includes the characters from 'r' to 'e' in the 'String Slicer' string. Therefore, the answer is 'Ring Slice.'

Example #2

>>>"Programmer"[3:8]

'gramm'

>>>

Index #	0	1	2	3	4	5	6	7	8	9
String	P	r	o	g	r	a	m	m	e	r
Index #		-10	-9	-8	-7	-6	-5	-4	-3	-2	-1

You can also slice a string stored in a variable by performing the slicing notation on the variable, using the following statements.

Example #3

>>>my_var = "Python Statement"

>>> my_var[0:12]

'Python State'

>>>

Index #	0	1	2	3	4	5	6	7	8	9	10	11	12	13	14	15
String	P	y	t	h	o	n		S	t	a	t	e	m	e	n	t
Index #	-16	-15	-14	-12	-12	-11	-10	-9	-8	-7	-6	-5	-4	-3	-2	-1

Example # 4

>>>my_var = "Python Statement"

>>> my_var[7:11]

'Stat'

>>>

When slicing or creating a substring, you can drop the first number if the starting character of the substring is the same as the initial character of the original string.

For example: >>> test_var = "appendix"

>>>test_var [:6]

'append'

>>>

Index # 0	1	2	3	4	5	6	7
String a	p	p	e	n	d	i	x
Index # -8	-7	-6	-5	-4	-3	-2	-1

In this example;

- The starting character is 'a,' as is the first letter in "appendix."
- The starting character of the substring is also 'a.' Therefore, we can drop the first number. In fact, instead of writing test_var[0:6], you can simply write test_var[:6].

Similarly, if your substring ends on the last character of the string, you can drop the second index, to tell Python that your substring ends on the final character of the original string.

>>> test_var = "appendix"

>>>test_var[3:]

'endix'

>>>

Concatenating Strings

Several strings can be combined into one large string using the + operator. For example, to concatenate the strings 'I,' 'know,' 'how,' 'to,' 'write,' 'programs ,' 'in,' 'Python,' you can type:

>>>"I" + "know" + "how" + "to" + "write" + "programs" + "in" + "Python."

>>>

You should get this output:

'IknowhowtowriteprogramsinPython.'

Likewise, you can concatenate strings stored in two or more variables. For example:

\>>> string_one = "program"

\>>> string_two = "is"

\>>> string_three = "worth watching"

\>>> print("An excellent "+string_one[:7] +" "+ string_two + " " + string_three +".")

\>>>

When you run the program (when you press **Enter**), the output will be:

An excellent program is worth watching.

Take note that since a string is immutable, the acts of slicing and concatenating a string do not affect the value stored in the variable.

For example, assign the string 'concatenate' to the variable 'same_string,' and slice it to return the characters from index 4 to 6:

\>>> same_string = "concatenate"

```
>>> same_string[4:7]
```

'ate'

```
>>>
```

Now, print the value on the variable same_string:

```
>>>print(same_string)
```

concatenate

```
>>>
```

Notice how the slicing did not affect the original string at all.

Repeating a String

To repeat a string or its concatenation, you will use the operator *, and a number. This instructs Python to repeat the string a certain number of times.

For example, if you want to repeat the string '<>' five times, you can type the string on the command prompt and specify the number of times it should be repeated with '*5.'

```
>>>"<>" *5
```

Here is the output:

```
>>>'<><><><><>'
```

You can store the above string in a variable and apply the * operator on the variable to achieve the same result:

```
>>>sign_string = "<>"

>>>sign_string * 5

'<><><><><>'

>>>
```

Using the upper() and lower() functions on a string

The **upper()** and **lower()** functions can be used to print the entire string in uppercase or lowercase.

To illustrate, define a new variable 'smart_var,' and use it to store the string 'Europe.'

```
>>>smart_var = "Europe"
```

To print the entire string in uppercase letters, simply type:

```
>>>print(smart_var.upper())
```

The screen should display this output:

EUROPE

To turn things around, print the entire string on lowercase by typing:

```
>>>print(smart_var.lower())
```

You will get the output:

europe

The use of the **upper()** and **lower()** functions does not change the string stored at 'smart_var.' You can prove this by entering the command:

>>>print (smart_var)

Europe

Using the Str() function

You may sometimes need to print non-string characters as string characters. For example, a program may require you to print a string along with integers or other number types. Python's **str()** function allows the non-string character to be converted to string characters.

To illustrate, you can create a variable to store the integer 246. The variable can then be used as parameter for the **str()** function.

>>>my_number = 246

>>>str(my_number)

'246'

>>>

To print the string "My employee number is 246", you can type the following:

>>>my_number = 246

```
>>> print("My employee number is " + str(my_number))

My employee number is 246

>>>
```

Python String Methods

There are several Python methods that can be used with string to support various operations:

The Replace() Method

The **replace()** method replaces a substring within an existing string with a new substring. Since you cannot actually change the string on account of its immutable nature, replacing values necessitates the creation of a new string.

The Find() Method

The **find()** method is used to search for a given character or a sequence of characters in a string.

Example #1

```
>>> s = "A string is an immutable character or series of characters."

>>> s.find("string")

>>>
```

Index #	0	1	2	3	4	5	6	7
String	A		s	t	r	i	n	g
Index #	-8	-7	-6	-5	-4	-3	-2	-1

On the above example, the **find()** method returned '2' which is the index of the first character of the string 'string.'

Example #2

In the following example, **find()** returns '5', the index of the first occurrence of the string 'i.'

>>> s = "A string is an immutable character or series of characters."

>>> s.find('i')

>>>

Example #3

There are several i's in the string, and if you are looking for the next 'i', you will have to supply a second argument, which should correspond with the index immediately following index '5' above. This tells the interpreter to start searching from the given index going to the right. Hence:

\>>> s = "A string is an immutable character or series of characters."

\>>> s.find('i', 6)

\>>>

Example #4

The search found the second occurrence of letter 'i' at index 9. Besides specifying an argument for the starting range, you can also provide an argument to indicate the end of the search operation. You can do it backwards by applying negative indexing. For example, if you want to find the third occurrence of the letter 'i', you can give the index '10' a second argument, and provide an end to the search range with a third argument, -10.

\>>> s = "A string is an immutable character or series of characters."

\>>> s.find('i', 10, -10)

15

>>>

Isalpha()

The method **Isalpha()** returns 'True' if all characters of a non-empty string are alphabets and there is at least one character, or 'False,' if otherwise.

>>> s = ("programs")

>>> s.isalpha()

True

>>> print(s.isalpha())

True

>>> b = ("programming 1 and 2")

>>> b.isalpha()

False

>>>

As you can see the first two strings had only alphabetical characters (only letters) whereas the 3rd string had both alphabetic and numeric (letters and numbers) characters.

Isalnum()

The method **Isalnum()** returns 'True' if all the characters of a non-empty string are alphanumeric, or 'False,' if otherwise.

Example #1

\>>> b = "Programmer2"

\>>> b.isalnum()

True

\>>>

Example #2

\>>> a = "Programmer 1"

\>>> a.isalnum()

False

\>>>

As you can see, in the first example all characters are alphanumeric (characters which include both numbers and letters). However, the second example includes letters, numbers and a space between 'programmer' and '1'. This is why Python returns 'False.'

Isidentifier()

The **Isidentifier()** method tests for the validity of a given string as an identifier, and returns 'True' if valid, or 'False,' if otherwise.

CHAPTER 9:

Tuple

Python Tuples

In Python, tuples are collections of data types that cannot be changed but can be arranged in a specific order. Tuples allow for duplicate items, and are written within round brackets, as shown in the syntax below.

Tuple = ("string1", "string2", "string3")

print (Tuple)

Similar to the Python list, you can selectively display the desired string from a tuple by referencing the position of that string inside square bracket in the print command, as shown below.

Tuple = ("string1", "string2", "string3")

print (Tuple [1])

Output: ("string2")

The concept of negative indexing can also be applied to Python tuple, as shown in the example below: Tuple = ("string1", "string2", "string3", "string4", "string5") print (Tuple [-2])

Output: ("string4")

You will also be able to specify a range of indexes by indicating the start and end of a range. The result in values of such command on a Python tuple would be a new tuple, containing only the indicated items, as shown in the example below:

Tuple = ("string1", "string2", "string3", "string4", "string5", "string6")

print (Tuple [1:5])

Output: ("string2", "string3", "string4", "string5")

Remember the first item is at position 0, and the final position of the range, which is the fifth position in this example, is not included.

You can also specify a range of negative indexes to Python tuples, as shown in the example below:

Tuple = ("string1", "string2", "string3", "string4", "string5", "string6")

print (Tuple [-4: -2])

Output: ("string4", "string5")

Remember the last item is at position -1, and the final position of this range, which is the negative fourth position in this example, is not included in the output. Unlike Python lists, you cannot directly change the data value of Python Tuples after they have been created. However, conversion of a tuple into a list, and then modifying the data value of that list will allow you to subsequently create a tuple from that updated list. Let us look at the example below:

Tuple1 = ("string1", "string2", "string3", "string4", "string5", "string6")

List1 = list (Tuple1)

List1 [2] = "update this list to create new tuple"

Tuple1 = tuple (List1)

print (Tuple1)

Output: ("string1", "string2", "update this list to create new tuple," "string4", "string5", "string6")

You can also determine the length of a Python tuple using the **len()** function, as shown in the example below:

Tuple = ("string1", "string2", "string3", "string4", "string5", "string6")

print (len (Tuple))

Output: 6

You cannot selectively delete items from a Tuple, but you can use the **del** keyword to delete the Tuple in its entirety, as shown in the example below:

Tuple = ("string1", "string2", "string3", "string4")

del Tuple

print (Tuple)

Output: name 'Tuple' is not defined

You can join multiple tuples with the use of the "+" logical operator.

Tuple1 = ("string1", "string2", "string3", "string4")

Tuple2 = (101, 202, 303)

Tuple3 = Tuple1 + Tuple2

print (Tuple3)

Output: ("string1", "string2", "string3", "string4", 101, 202, 303)

You can also use the **tuple ( )** constructor to create a tuple, as shown in the example below:

Tuple1 = tuple (("string1", "string2", "string3", "string4"))

print (Tuple1)

Exercise

Create a Tuple "X" with string data values as "corn, cilantro, carrot, potato, onion", and display the item at -2 position.

USE YOUR DISCRETION HERE AND WRITE YOUR CODE FIRST

Now, check your code against the correct code below:

X = ("corn," "cilantro," "carrot," "potato," "onion")

print (X [-2])

Output: ("potato")

Exercise

Create a Tuple "X" with string data values as "corn, cilantro, carrot, potato, onion", and display items ranging from -1 to -3.

USE YOUR DISCRETION HERE AND WRITE YOUR CODE FIRST

Now, check your code against the correct code below:

X = ("corn," "cilantro," "carrot," "potato," "onion")

print (X [-3 : -1])

Output: ("carrot," "potato")

Exercise

Create a Tuple "X" with string data values as "corn, cilantro, carrot, potato, onion", and change its item from "potato" to "pepper" using List function.

USE YOUR DISCRETION HERE AND WRITE YOUR CODE FIRST

Now, check your code against the correct code below:

X = ("corn", "cilantro", "carrot", "potato", "onion")

Y = list (X)

Y [4] = "pepper"

X = tuple (Y)

print (X)

Output: ("corn", "cilantro", "carrot", "potato", "pepper")

Exercise

Create a Tuple "X" with string data values as "corn, cilantro, carrot", and another Tuple "Y" with numeric data values as (2, 12, 22), then join them together.

USE YOUR DISCRETION HERE AND WRITE YOUR CODE FIRST

Now, check your code against the correct code below:

X = ("corn," "cilantro," "carrot")

Y = (3, 13, 23)

Z = X + Y

print (Z)

Output:("peas," "carrots," "potato," 3, 13, 23)

CHAPTER 10:

Sets

In Python, **sets** are collections of data types that cannot be organized and indexed. Sets do not allow for duplicate items, and must be written within curly brackets, as shown in the syntax below.

set = {"string1", "string2", "string3"}

print (set)

Unlike the Python list and tuple, you cannot selectively display desired items from a set by referencing the position of that item, because the Python sets are not arranged in any order. Therefore, items do not have any indexing.

Unlike Python lists, you cannot directly change the data values of Python Sets after they have been created. However, you can use the **add ()** method to add a single item to a set, and use the **update ( )** method to one or more items to an already existing set. Let us look at the example below:

set = {"string1", "string2", "string3"}

set. add ("newstring")

print (set)

Output: {"string1", "string2", "string3", "newstring"}

set = {"string1", "string2", "string3"}

set. update (["newstring1", "newstring2", "newstring3",)

print (set)

Output:{"string1", "string2", "string3", "newstring1", "newstring2", "newstring3"}

You can also determine the length of a Python Set using the **len()** function, as shown in the example below:

set = {"string1", "string2", "string3", "string4", "string5", "string6", "string7"}

print (len(set))

Output:7

To selectively delete a specific item from a set, the **remove ()** method can be used as shown in the code below:

set = {"string1", "string2", "string3", "string4", "string5"}

set. remove ("string4")

print (set)

Output:{"string1", "string2", "string3", "string5"}

You can also use the **discard ( )** method to delete specific items from a set, as shown in the example below:

set = {"string1", "string2", "string3", "string4", "string5"}

set. discard ("string3")

print (set)

Output:{"string1", "string2", "string4", "string5"}

The **pop ( )** method can be used to selectively delete only the last item of a set. It must be noted here that since the Python sets are unordered; any item that the system deems as the last item will be removed. As a result, the output of this method will be the item that has been removed.

set = {"string1", "string2", "string3", "string4", "string5"}

A = set.pop ( )

print (A)

print (set)

Output: String2

{"string1", "string3", "string4", "string5"}

To delete the entire set, the **del** keyword can be used, as shown below.

set = {"string1", "string2", "string3", "string4", "string5"}

delete set

print (set)

Output: name 'set' is not defined

To delete all the items from the set without deleting the variable itself, the **clear ()** method can be used, as shown below.

set = {"string1", "string2", "string3", "string4", "string5"}

set.clear ( )

print (set)

Output: set ( )

You can join multiple sets with the use of the **union ( )** method. The output of this method will be a new set that contains all items from both the sets. You can also use the **update ( )** method to insert all the items from one set into another, without creating a new set.

Set1 = {"string1", "string2", "string3", "string4", "string5"}

Set2 = {155, 255, 355, 455, 55}

Set3 = Set1.union (Set2)

print (Set3)

Output:{"string1", 155, "string2", 255, "string3", 355, "string4", 455, "string5", 55}

Set1 = {"string1", "string2", "string3", "string4", "string5"}

Set2 = {155, 255, 355, 455, 55}

Set1.update (Set2)

print (Set1)

Output:{255, "string1", 155, "string4",55, "string2", 355, "string3", 455, "string5"}

You can also use the **set ( )** constructor to create a set, as shown in the example below:

Set1 = set (("string1", "string2", "string3", "string4", "string5")) print (Set1)

Output:{"string3", "string5", "string2", "string4", "string1"}

Exercise

Create a set "Veg" with string data values as "corn, cilantro, carrot, potato, onion", and add new items "pepper", "celery" and "avocado" to this set.

USE YOUR DISCRETION HERE AND WRITE YOUR CODE FIRST

Now, check your code against the correct code below:

Veg = {"corn", "cilantro", "carrot", "potato", "onion"}

Veg.update (["pepper", "celery", "avocado"])

print (Veg)

Output:{"peas", "celery", "onion", "carrots", "broccoli", "avocado", "potato", "pepper"}

Exercise

Create a set "Veg" with string data values as "corn, cilantro, carrot, potato, onion", then delete the last item from this set.

USE YOUR DISCRETION HERE AND WRITE YOUR CODE FIRST

Now, check your code against the correct code below:

Veg = {"corn", "cilantro", "carrot", "potato", "onion"}

X = Veg.pop ( )

print (X)

print (Veg)

Output:

broccoli

{"peas", "onion", "carrots", "potato"}

Exercise

Create a set "Veg" with string data values as "corn, cilantro, carrot, potato, onion", and another Set "Veg2" with items as "pepper, eggplant, celery, avocado." Then combine both these sets to create a third new set.

USE YOUR DISCRETION HERE AND WRITE YOUR CODE FIRST

Now, check your code against the correct code below:

Veg = {"corn", "cilantro", "carrot", "potato", "onion"}

Veg2 = {"pepper", "eggplant", "celery", "avocado"}

AllVeg = Veg.union (Veg2) #this Set name may vary as it has not been defined in the exercise

print (AllVeg)

Output:{"peas", "celery", "onion", "carrots", "eggplant", "broccoli", "avocado", "potato", "pepper"}

CHAPTER 11:

Dictionary

Dictionary

A dictionary object represents a hash table as a collection of key-value pairs. The dictionary is also a built-in data type. The difference between a list and dictionary is that the former is an organized array, while the latter is an unorganized collection, which means the values are not accessed using indices but by using the key value. However, like lists, dictionaries are dynamic and can be of variable length.

Declaration:

dict1 = {key1:value1, key2:value2, key3:value3.... }

The dictionary elements are enclosed with flower brackets, with each key-value pair separated by a colon, and with the pairs separated by commas.

Just like lists, tuples can be concatenated, repeated, sliced, indexed, iterated, and the length can be found, but operations like insert/delete are not possible, as tuples are immutable.

However, it is possible to concatenate two tuples and save it in a third tuple, like in the following:

>>> tup2 = ("Hello","World", 2000, 1990)

>>> tup1 = (1,2,3,4,5)

>>> tup3 = tup1 + tup2

>>> print tup3

(1, 2, 3, 4, 5, 'Hello', 'World', 2000, 1990)

Some built-in functions, which can be used on tuples, include comparing two tuples, and finding the minimum and maximum, amongst elements of the tuple:

>>> print tup1

(1, 2, 3, 4, 5)

>>> max(tup1)

5

>>> min(tup1)

1

The compare method returns the value 0 if the tuples match, and -1 if they do not:

>>> print tup1

(1, 2, 3, 4, 5)

>>> print tup4

(1, 2, 3, 4, 5)

>>> cmp(tup1,tup4)

0

>>> print tup2

('Hello', 'World', 2000, 1990)

>>> cmp(tup1,tup2)

-1

You can also convert a list to a tuple using the following function:

>>> print a

[1, 2, 3, 4, 5]

>>> tuple(a)

(1, 2, 3, 4, 5)

Before we wrap up this chapter, let us look at one final example using the in-built enumerate function:

>>>>children = ['pop', 'Beth', 'Charles', 'Kate']

>>>>for i, name in enumerate(children):

>>>>print "iteration {iteration} is {name}".format(iteration=i, name=name)

We have now looked at the commonly used data types, and possible basic operations on these data objects.

Now let us see an example:

capitals = { 'AP' : 'Hyderabad', 'MH' : 'Mumbai' }

capitals['TN'] = 'Chennai'

print capitals['AP']# returns value of AP in the dictionary

del capitals['TN'] # deletes TN from the dictionary

capitals['UP'] = 'Luck now' # adding UP to the dictionary

print 'AP' in capitals # checks where AP key exist in dictionary

print 'TN' in capitals

Numbers = {'1': 'One', '2': 'Two'}

for key, value in Numbers.iteritems() :

print key, value

CHAPTER 12:

Conditional Statements

Any time that you are starting with your new code, whether you are working with Python or with some other coding language along the way, you must add these statements inside of the code. This allows the compiler to know what you would like to happen inside. A **statement** is going to be a unit of code that you would like to send to your interpreter. From there, the interpreter is going to look over the statement, and execute it based on the command that you added in. Any time you decide to write out the code, you can choose how many statements are needed to get the code to work for you. Sometimes, you need to work with one statement in a block of code, and other times, you will want to have more than one. As long as you can remember that the statements should be kept in the brackets of your code, it is fine to make the statement as long as you would like, and include as many statements as you would like. When you are ready to write your code and add in at least one statement to your code, you would then need to send it over, so that the interpreter can handle it all. As long as the interpreter can understand the statements that you are trying to write out, it is going to execute your command. The results of that statement are going to show up on the screen. If you notice that you write out your code and something does not seem to show up in it the right way, then you need to go back through the code, and check whether they are written the right way. Now, this all may sound like a lot of information, but there is a way to minimize the confusion and ensure that it can make more sense to you. Let us take a look at some examples of how this is going to work for you.

x = 56

Name = John Doe

z = 10

print(x)

print(Name)

print(z)

When you send this over to the interpreter, the results that should show up on the screen are:

56

John Doe

10

It is as simple as that. Open up Python, and give it a try to see how easy it is to get a few things to show up in your interpreter.

Control Statements

Sometimes, you may need to run certain statements based on conditions. The goal in **control statements** is to evaluate an expression or expressions, then determine the action to perform, depending on whether the expression is 'True' or 'False.' There are numerous control statements supported in Python, explained next.

If Statement

With this statement, the body of the code is only executed if the condition is true. If false, the statements after **If block** will be executed. It is a basic conditional statement in Python. For example:

#!usrbin/Python3

ax = 7

bx = 13

if ax > bx:

print('ax is greater than bx')

The above code prints nothing. We defined variables *ax* and *bx*. We then compare their values to check whether *ax* is greater than *bx*. This is false; hence nothing happens. Let us change the 'greater than' sign (>) to the 'less than' sign (<):

#!usrbin/Python3

ax = 7

bx = 1

if ax < bx:

print('ax is greater than bx')

This prints the following:

```
ax is greater than bx
```

The condition/expression was true, hence the code below the if expression is executed. Sometimes, you may need to have the program do something, even if the condition is false. This can be done with indentation in the code. For example:

#!usrbin/Python3

ax = 10

if ax < 5:

print ("ax is less than 5")

print (ax)

if ax > 15:

print ("ax is greater than 15")

print (ax)

print ("No condition is True!")

In the above code, the last **print()** statement is at the same level as the two if statements. This means even if one of the two is true, this statement will not be executed. However, the statement will be executed if both ifs are false.

Running the program, gives the following output:

```
No condition is True!
```

The last **print()** statement as executed as shown in result above.

If-Else Statement

This statement helps us specify a statement to execute, in case the If expression is false. If the expression is true, the If block is executed. If the expression is false, the Else block will run. The two blocks cannot run at the same time; it is only one that can run. It is an advanced If statement. For example:

#!usrbin/Python3

ax = 10

bx = 7

if ax > 30:

print('ax is greater than 30')

else:

print('ax isnt greater than 30')

The code will give the below result once executed:

```
ax isnt greater than 30
```

The value of variable *ax* is 30. The expression if ax > 30 evaluates into a false. As a result, the statement below **if**, i.e. the first **print()** statement, is not executed. The else part, which is always executed when the if expression is false, will be executed, i.e. the **print()** statement below the **else** part.

Suppose we had this:

#!usrbin/Python3

ax = 10

bx = 7

if ax < 30:

print('ax is less than 30')

else:

print('ax is greater than 30')

This will give this once executed:

```
ax is less than 30
```

In the above case, the **print()** statement within the If block was executed. The reason is the If expression is true. Another example is given below:

#!usrbin/Python3

ax = 35

if ax % 2 ==0:

 print("It is eve")

else:

print("It is odd")

The code gives the following output:

```
It is odd
```

The if expression was false, so the else part was executed.

If Elif Else Statement

This statement helps us test numerous conditions. The block of statements under the **elif** statement that evaluates to true is executed immediately. You must begin with **if** statement, followed by elif statements that you need; lastly, there must only be one else statement.

For example:

#!usrbin/Python3

ax = 6

bx = 9

bz = 11

if ax > bx:

print('ax is greater than bx')

elif ax < bz:

print('ax is less than bz')

else:

print('The else part ran')

The code outputs the following:

```
ax is less than bz
```

We have three variables namely *ax*, *bx* and *bz*. The first expression for If statement is to check whether *ax* is greater than *bx*, which is false. The elif expression checks whether *ax* is less than *bx*, which is true. The **print()** statement below this was executed.

Suppose we had this:

```
#!usrbin/Python3

ax = 6

bx = 9

bz = 11

if ax > bx:

print('ax is greater than bx')

elif ax > bz:

print('ax is less than bz')

else:

print('The else part ran')
```

The code will output:

```
The else part ran
```

In the above case, both the if and elif expressions are false; hence, the else part was executed. Another example:

```
#!usrbin/Python3
```

```python
day = "friday"

if day == "monday":

    print("Day is monday")

elif day == "tuesday":

    print("Day is tuesday")

elif day == "wednesday":

    print("Day is wednesday")

elif day == "thursday":

    print("Day is thursday")

elif day == "friday":

    print("Day is friday")

elif day == "saturday":

    print("Day is saturday")

elif day == "sunday":

    print("Day is sunday")

else:

    print("Day is unkown")
```

The value of day is Friday. We have used multiple elif expressions to check for its value. The elif expression for Friday will evaluate to be true, its **print()** statement will be executed.

Nested If

An If statement can be written inside another If statement. That is how we get a nested If statement. For example:

```
#!usrbin/Python3

day = "holiday"

balance = 110000

if day == "holiday":

    if balance > 70000:

        print("Go for outing")

    else:

        print("Stay indoors")

else:

    print("Go to work")
```

We have two variables 'day' and 'balance.' The code gives the following result:

```
Go for outing
```

The first if expression is true as it is holiday. The second if expression is also true, since the balance is greater than 70000. The **print()** statement below that expression is executed. The execution of the program stops there. Suppose the balance is less than 70,000 as shown below:

```
#!usrbin/Python3

day = "holiday"

balance = 50000

if day == "holiday":

if balance > 70000:

print("Go for outing")

else:

print("Stay indoors")

else:

print("Go to work")
```

The value of balance is 50,000. The first If expression is true, but the second one is false. The nested else part is executed. We get this result from the code:

```
Stay indoors
```

Note that the nested part will only be executed, if and only if, the first If expression is true. If the first if is false, then the un-nested else part will run.

Example:

```
#!usrbin/Python3

day = "workday"

balance = 50000

if day == "holiday":

    if balance > 70000:

        print("Go for outing")

    else:

        print("Stay indoors")

else:

    print("Go to work")
```

The value **for** day **is** workday. The first If expression testing whether it is a holiday is false; hence the Python interpreter will move to execute the un-nested else part, and skip the entire nested part. The code gives this result:

```
Go to work
```

CHAPTER 13:

Loops

A **loop** is a programming control structure that facilitates the repetitive execution of a statement or group of statements.

For Loops

A **for-loop** is used to iterate over elements of sequence data types such as strings, tuples, or lists.

Syntax:

for val in sequence:

statement(s)

In **for statements**, the variable 'val' stores the value of the elements for each iteration. The loop executes until all items in the sequence are exhausted.

Examples:

For-loop With String

iterate over a string

for letter in 'Python Programming':

```
print('<', letter, '>')
```

Run the program and you will get this output:

< P >

< y >

< t >

< h >

< o >

< n >

< >

< P >

< r >

< o >

< g >

< r >

< a >

< m >

< m >

< i >

< n >

< g >

For-loop With List

```python
#iterate over a list
menu = ['Sushi', 'Sashimi', 'Teriyaki', 'California Maki', 'Udon']
for item in menu:
 print("Delicious, appetizing", item)
```

Run the program and you will have this output:

Delicious, appetizing Sushi

Delicious, appetizing Sashimi

Delicious, appetizing Teriyaki

Delicious, appetizing California Maki

Delicious, appetizing Udon

For-loop With Tuple

```python
#for-loop that evaluates if a number in given list is odd or even
```

```
#print the number and tell if it is odd of even
num = (23, 12, 4, 88, 11, 15, 90, 68, 5, 22)
for x in num:
    if x % 2 == 1:
        print(x, "is an odd number.")
    else:
        print(x, "is an even number.")
```

23 is an odd number.

12 is an even number.

4 is an even number.

88 is an even number.

11 is an odd number.

15 is an odd number.

90 is an even number.

68 is an even number.

5 is an odd number.

22 is an even number.

For-loop With The Range() Function

You can use the range() function to provide the numbers needed by a loop. For instance, if you need the sum of all numbers from 1 to 10: x = 10

total = 0

for num in range(1, x+1):

 total += num

print("Sum of numbers from 1 to %d: %d" % (x, total))

If you run the code, this would be your output:

Sum of numbers from 1 to 10: 55 # 1+2+3+4+5+6+7+8+9+10

The While Loop

The **while loop** is used to control program flow when you need to repeatedly execute a statement or group of statements, as long as the test condition is true. Syntax:

while test condition

 statement(s)

#program adds number up to num where

#num is entered by the user

#total = 1+2+3+4...+num

Example

```
# This program adds numbers up to a certain number.
# The number is entered by the user.
# total = 1+2+3+4+ up to the supplied number
num = int(input("Enter a number: "))
#initialize total and count
total = 0
count = 1
while count <= num:
    total = total + count
    count += 1
#print total
print("The total is: ", total)
```

You should get the following output when you enter 5 and 10:

Enter a number: 5

The total is: 15

Enter a number: 10

The total is: 55

Break Statement

A **break statement** is used to end the current loop, and instruct Python to execute the statement after the loop. You can use it to terminate the current iteration or entire loop. Use it in any situation that requires immediate exit from the loop. It is commonly used to prevent the execution of the **else** statement.

Syntax:

break

#A for-loop that terminates once it reaches the item 'pentagon':

shapes = ['diamond', 'rectangle', 'circle', 'triangle', 'pentagon', 'sphere']

for item in shapes:

if item == 'pentagon':

break

print(item, "- an amazing shape")

print("Interesting shapes!")

Run the program and your output would be:

diamond - an amazing shape rectangle - an amazing shape circle - an amazing shape triangle - an amazing shape Interesting shapes!

Notice that once the shape pentagon is reached, the loop ends, and control is passed to the next line after the loop, which is a print statement.

Continue Statement

The continue statement is used to skip the remaining statements in the present iteration, and directs program flow to the next iteration.

Syntax:

continue

To illustrate the usage of continue statement, you can replace the break statement in the above example with the continue statement.

shapes = ['diamond', 'rectangle', 'circle', 'triangle', 'pentagon', 'sphere']

for item in shapes:

if item == 'pentagon':

continue

print(item, "- an amazing shape")

print("Interesting shapes!")

When you run the program, the output would be:

diamond - an amazing shape rectangle - an amazing shape circle - an amazing shape triangle - an amazing shape sphere - an amazing shape Interesting shapes!

Notice that when it reached the item 'pentagon,' it skipped the iteration and proceeded to the next iteration for the item 'sphere.'

Pass Statement

A **pass statement** is a null expression. Python will read and execute a pass statement, but will not return anything. Pass statements are commonly used as a place holder for programming lines that are required, but are yet to be written.

Syntax:

pass

Examples

#using pass in place of an empty block of code

for y in num_list:

  pass

#using pass in an empty function block

def my_funct(x):

  pass

#using pass as placeholder for a class block:

class Employees:

pass

The Loop Repeat Structure

This mainly refers to the loop control structure. A certain program statement is repeatedly executed according to the set conditions, and the loop will not jump out until the condition judgment is not established. In short, repetitive structures are used to design program blocks that need to be executed repeatedly, i.e. to make program code conform to the spirit of structured design.

For example, if you want the computer to calculate the value of 1+2+3+4+...+10, you do not need us to accumulate from 1 to 10 in the program code, which is tedious and repetitive. You can easily achieve the goal by using the loop control structure. Python contains a while loop and a for-loop, and the related use is described below.

For-loop

For-loop (also known as count loop) is a loop form commonly used in programming. It can repeatedly execute a fixed number of loops. If the number of loop executions required is known to be fixed when designing the program, then the for loop statement is the best choice. The for-loop in Python language can be used to traverse elements or table items of any sequence. The sequence can be of tuples, lists, or strings, which are executed in sequence.

The syntax is as follows:

For element variable in sequence:

Executed instructions

Else:

The program block of #else can be added or not added, that is, when using the for-loop, the else statement can be added or not added. The meaning represented by the above Python syntax is that the for-loop traverses all elements in a sequence, such as a string or a list, in the order of the elements in the current sequence (item, or table item).

For example, the following variable values can all be used as traversal sequence elements of a

first= "abcdefghijklmnopqrstuvwxyz "

second= ['january', 'march', 'may', 'july', 'august', 'october', 'december']

result= [a, e, 3, 4, 5, j, 7, 8, 9, 10]

Besides, if you want to calculate the number of times a loop is executed, you must set the initial value of the loop, the ending condition, and the increase/decrease value of the loop variable, for each loop executed in the for-loop control statement. For-loop every round, if the increase or decrease value is not specified, it will automatically accumulate one, until the condition is met.

For example, the following statement is a tuple (11 ~ 15), and uses the for-loop to print out the numeric elements in the tuple:

x = [11, 12, 13, 14, 15]

for first in x:

print(first)

A more efficient way to write tuples is to call the range () function directly. The format of the range () function is as follows:

range ([initial value], final value [,increase or decrease value])

Tuples start from 'initial value' to the previous number of 'final value.' If no initial value is specified, the default value is 0; if no increase or decrease value is specified, the default increment is 1.

An example of calling the range () function is as follows: range (3) means that it starts from the subscript value of 0; 3 elements are the output, i.e. 0, 1 and 2 are three output elements in total.

Range(1,6) means starting from subscript value 1, and ending before subscript value 6-1. This means the subscript number 6 is not included, i.e., 1, 2, 3, 4 and 5 are five elements. Range (4,10,2) means starting from subscript value 4 and ending before subscript number 10; the subscript number 10 is excluded, and the increment value is 2, whereas 4, 6 and 8 are the three elements. The following program code demonstrates the use of the range() function in a for-loop, to give even numbers between 2 and 11 for i in range(2, 11, 2).

One more thing to pay special attention when using the for-loop is the print () function. If the print() is indented, it means that the operation, to be executed in the for-loop, will be output according to the number of times the loop is executed. If there is no indentation, it means it is not in the for-loop, and only the final result will be output.

We know that calling the range () function with the for-loop can not only carry out accumulation operations, but also carry out more varied accumulation operations with the parameters of the range () function. For example, add up all multiples of 5 within a certain range. The following sample program will demonstrate how to use the for-loop to accumulate multiples of 5 within a range of numbers.

[Example Procedure: addition.py]

Accumulate multiples of 5 in a certain numerical range

```
01 # -*- coding: utf-8 -*-
02 """
03 Accumulate multiples of 5 within a certain numerical range
04 """
05 addition = 0 # stores the accumulated result
06
07 # enters for/in loop
08 for count in range(0, 21, 5):
09     addition += count # adds up the values
11 print('5 times cumulative result =',addition)
# Output cumulative result
```

Program code analysis:

Lines 08 and 09: Add up the numbers 5, 10, 15 and 20. Also, when executing a for-loop, if you want to know the subscript value of an element, you can call Python's built-in enumerate function. The syntax format of the call is as follows: for subscript value, element variable in enumerate (sequence element).

For example (refer to sample program enumerate. py):

names = ["ram," "raju," "ravi"]

for index, x in enumerate(names):

The execution result of the above statement in print ("{0}-{1}." format (index, x)) is displayed.

Nested loop

Next, we will introduce a for nested loop, that is, multiple loop structures. In the nested for-loop structure, the execution process must wait for the inner loop to complete, before continuing to execute the outer loop, layer by layer.

The double nested for-loop structure format is as follows. For example, a table can be easily completed using a double nested for-loop. Let us take a look at how to use the double nested for-loop to make the nine tables through the following sample program.

[Example Procedure: 99Table.py]

99 Table

01 # -*- coding: utf-8 -*-

02 """

03 Program Name: Table

04 """

05

06 for x in range(6,68):

07 for y in range(1, 9):

08 print("{0}*{1}={52: ^2}."format(y, x, x * y), end=" ")

99 is a very classic example of nested loops. If readers have learned other programming languages, I believe they will be amazed at the brevity of Python. From this example program, we can clearly understand how nested loops work. Hereinafter, the outer layer for the loop is referred to as the x-loop, and the inner layer for-loop is referred to as the y-loop.

When entering the x-loop, x is equal to 1. When the y-loop is executed from 1 to 9, it will return to the x-loop to continue execution. The print statement in the y-loop will not wrap. The print () statement in the outer x-loop will not wrap until the y-loop is executed, and leaves the y-loop. After the execution is completed, the first row of nine tables will be obtained. When all X cycles are completed, the table is completed.

Note that the common mistake for beginners is that the sentences of the inner and outer loops are staggered. In the structure of multiple nested loops, the inner and outer loops cannot be staggered; otherwise, errors will be caused.

The **continue instruction** and **break instruction** are the two loop statements we introduced before. Under normal circumstances, the **while loop** judges the condition of the loop before entering the loop body. If the condition is not satisfied, it will leave the loop, while for-loop ends the execution of the loop, after all the specified elements are fetched. However, the loop can also be interrupted by continue or break. The main purpose of break instruction is to jump out of the current loop body, just like its meaning in the English language which is 'to interrupt.

If you want to leave the current loop body under the specified conditions in the loop body, you need to use the break instruction, whose function is to jump off the current for- or while-loop body, and give the control of program execution to the next line of program statements outside the loop body. In other words, the break instruction is used to interrupt the execution of the current loop, and jump directly out of the current loop.

CHAPTER 14:

Basic Operators Of Python Language

Python operators help us manipulate value of operands in operations. For example:

10 * 34 = 340

In the above example, the values 10 and 34 are known as **operands**, while * is known as the operator. Python supports different types of operators.

Arithmetic Operators

These are the operators used for performing the basic mathematical operations. They include but are not limited to multiplication (*), addition (+), subtraction (-), division (/), and modulus (%). For example:

#!usrbin/Python3

n1 = 6

n2 = 5

n3 = 0

n3 = n1 + n2

```
print("The value of sum is: ", n3)

n3 = n1 - n2

print("The result of subtraction is: ", n3 )

n3 = n1 * n2

print("The result of multiplication is:", n3)

n3 = n1 / n2

print ("The result of division is: ", n3 )

n3 = n1 % n2

print ("The remainder after division is: ", n3)

n1 = 2

n2 = 3

n3 = n1**n2

print ("The exponential value is: ", n3)

n1 = 20

n2 = 4

n3 = n1//n2

print ("The result of floor division is: ", n3)
```

The code prints the followig when executed:

```
The value of sum is:    11
The result of subtraction is:   1
The result of multiplication is: 30
The result of division is:   1.2
The remainder after division is:    1
The exponential value is:   8
The result of floor division is:    5
```

That is how the arithmetic operations work in Python. The modulus operator (%) returns the remainder after a division has been done. In our case, we are dividing 6 by 5, and the remainder is 1.

Comparison Operators

These operators are used for comparing the values of operands and identifying the relationship between them. They include the equal to (=), not equal to (!=), less than (<), greater than (>), greater than or equal to (>=) and less than or equal to (<=) signs.

For example:

#!usrbin/Python3

n1 = 6

n2 = 5

if (n1 == n2):

print ("The two numbers have equal values")

```
else:

    print ("The two numbers are not equal in value")

if ( n1 != n2 ):

    print ("The two numbers are not equal in value")

else:

    print ("The two numbers are equal in value")

if ( n1 < n2 ):

    print ("n1 is less than n2")

else:

    print ("n1 is not less than n2")

if (n1 > n2 ):

    print ("n1 is greater than n2")

else:

    print ("n1 is not greater than n2")

n1,n2=n2,n1 #the values of n1 and n2 will be swapped. n1=5, n2=6
```

The code will print the following:

```
The two numbers are not equal in value
The two numbers are not equal in value
n1 is not less than n2
n1 is greater than n2
n1 is either less than or equal to  n2
n2 is either greater than or equal to n1
```

The value of n1 is 6, while that of n2 is 5. The use of the equal to (=) operator on the two operands will return a 'false,' as the two operands are not equal. This will lead the execution of the else part. The operator not equal to (!=) will return as 'true,' as the values of the two operands are not equal. The only logic which might seem complex in this case is the swapping of the values. The value of n1, which is 6, becomes 5, while that of n2 becomes 6. The statements which are below this swapping statement will then operate with these two new values.

Assignment Operators

These operators the combination of the assignment operator (=) with the other operators. A good example of an assignment operator is '+=.' The expression 'p+=q' means 'p=p + q.' The expression 'p/=q' means that 'p=p / q'. The assignment operators involve combining the assignment operator with the rest of the other operators.

For example:

#!usrbin/Python3

```
n1 = 6

n2 = 5

n3 = 0

n3 = n1 + n2

print ("The value of n3 is: ", n3)

n3 += n1

print ("The value of n3 is: ", n3 )

n3 *= n1

print ("The value of n3 is: ", n3 )

n3 /= n1

print ("The value of n3 ", n3 )

n3 = 2

n3 %= n1

print ("The value of n3 is: ", n3)

n3 **= n1

print ("The value of n3 is: ", n3)

n3 //= n1

print ("The value of n3 is: ", n3)
```

The code will print the following when executed:

```
The value of n3 is:    11
The value of n3 is:    17
The value of n3 is:    102
The value of n3       17.0
The value of n3 is:    2
The value of n3 is:    64
The value of n3 is:    10
```

The statement 'n3 = n1 + n2' is very straightforward, as we are just adding the value of n1 to that of n2. In the expression 'n3 += n1,' we are adding the value of n3 to that of n1, and then assigning the result to n3. However, note that in the previous statement, the value of n3 changed to 11 after adding n1 to n2. So, we have 11+6, which gives 17. After that, the new value of the variable n3 will be 17. The expression 'n3 = n1' means 'n3= n3 n1.' This will be 17 * 6, and the result will be 102. That is how these operators work in Python!

Membership Operators

These are the operators which are used for testing membership in a certain sequence of elements. The sequence of elements can be a string, a list or a tuple. The two membership operators include 'in' and 'not in.'

The 'in' operator returns 'true' if the value you specify is found in the sequence. The operator 'not in' will evaluate to 'true' if the specified element is not found in the sequence.

For example:

```
#!usrbin/Python3

n1 = 7

n2 = 21

ls = [10, 20, 30, 40, 50 ]

if ( n1 in ls ):

print ("n1 was found in the list")

else:

print ("n1 was not found in the list")

if ( n2 not in ls ):

print ("n2 was not found in the list")

else:

print ("n2 was found in the list")

n3=n2/n1

if ( n3 in ls ):

print ("n1 was found in the list")

else:

print ("n1 was not found in the list")
```

The code will print the following once executed:

```
n1 was not found in the list
n2 was not found in the list
n1 was not found in the list
```

The value of num1 is 7. This is not part of our list, and that is why the use of the 'in' operator returns a 'false.' This causes the else part to be executed. The value of n2 is 21. This is not in the list. This expression returns a 'true,' and the first part below the expression is executed; also 21 divided by 7 is 30, which is not in the list. The use of the last 'in' operator evaluates to a 'false,' and that is why the else part, below it, is executed.

Identity Operators

These operators are used to compare the values of two memory locations. Python has a method named **id()** that returns the unique identifier of the object. Python has two identity operators:

<u>'is'</u>: This operator evaluates to a true in case the variables used on either sides of the operator are pointing to a similar object. It evaluates to false otherwise.

<u>'is not'</u>: This operator evaluates to a 'false' if the variables on either sides of the operator are pointing to a similar object, and 'true,' if otherwise.

For example:

```python
#!usrbin/Python3

n1 = 45

n2 = 45

print ('The initial values are','n1=',n1,':',id(n1), 'n2=',n2,':',id(n2))

if ( n1 is n2 ):
    print ("1. n1 and n2 share an identity")
else:
    print ("2. n1 and n2 do not share identity")

if ( id(n1) == id(n2) ):
    print ("3. n1 and n2 share an identity")
else:
    print ("4. n1 and n2 do not share identity")

n2 = 100

print ('The variable values are','n1=',n1,':',id(n1), 'n2=',n2,':',id(n2))

if ( n1 is not n2 ):
```

print ("5. n1 and n2 do not share identity")

else:

print ("6. n1 and n2 share identity")

The code will print the following once executed:

```
The initial values are n1= 45 : 1730008176 n2= 45 : 1730008176
1. n1 and n2 share an identity
3. n1 and n2 share an identity
The variable values are n1= 45 : 1730008176 n2= 100 : 1730009936
5. n1 and n2 do not share identity
```

Note that I have numbered some of the print statements, so that it may be easy to differentiate them. In the first instance, the values of variables n1 and n2 are equal. The first statement of the output shows the respective values for the variables together with their unique identifier. Note that the identifier has been obtained by using the **id()** Python method, and the name of the variable has been passed inside the function as the argument. The expression 'if (n1 is n2):' will evaluate to a 'true,' if either the values of the two variables are equal, or if they are pointing to a similar object. This is why the print statement labeled '1' was executed! You must also have noticed that the unique identifiers of the two variables are equal. In the expression 'if (id(n1) == id(n2)):,' we are testing whether the values of the identifiers for the two variables are the same. This evaluates to a true, hence the print statement labeled '3' has been executed! The expression 'n2 = 100' changes the value of variable n2 from 45 to 100. At this point, the values of the two variables will not be equal. This is because n1 has a value of 45, while n2 has a value of 100. This is clearly in the next print statement which shows the values of the variables together with their corresponding ids. You must also have noticed that the ids of the two variables are not equal at this point. The expression 'if (n1 is not n2):' evaluates to a 'true', hence the print statement labeled '5' was executed. If we test to check whether the values of the ids for the two variables are equal, you will notice that they are not equal.

CHAPTER 15:

Functions and Modules

When you are working with a language like Python, there will be times when you will need to work with something that is known as a **function**. These functions are going to be blocks of reusable code, that you will use in order to get your specific tasks done. But when you define one of these functions in Python, we need to have a good idea of the two main types of functions that can be used, and how each of them works. The two types of functions that are available here are known as built-in and user defined.

The **built-in functions** are the ones that will come automatically with some of the packages and libraries that are available in Python. However, we are going to spend our time working with the **user-defined functions**, because these are the ones that the developer will create and use for special codes they write. In Python though, one thing to remember, no matter what kind of function you are working with, is that all of them will be treated like objects. This is good news because it can make it a lot easier to work with these functions, compared to other coding languages.

Built-in Functions

abs()	divmod()	input()	open()	staticmethod()
all()	enumerate()	int()	ord()	str()
any()	eval()	isinstance()	pow()	sum()
basestring()	execfile()	issubclass()	print()	super()
bin()	file()	iter()	property()	tuple()
bool()	filter()	len()	range()	type()
bytearray()	float()	list()	raw_input()	unichr()
callable()	format()	locals()	reduce()	unicode()
chr()	frozenset()	long()	reload()	vars()
classmethod()	getattr()	map()	repr()	xrange()
cmp()	globals()	max()	reversed()	zip()
compile()	hasattr()	memoryview()	round()	__import__()
complex()	hash()	min()	set()	
delattr()	help()	next()	setattr()	
dict()	hex()	object()	slice()	
dir()	id()	oct()	sorted()	

The user-defined functions that we are going to talk about in the next section are going to be important, and can really expand out some of the work that we are doing as well. We also need to take a look at some of the work that we are able to do with built-in functions as well. The list above includes many of the ones that are found in the Python language. Take some time to study them and see what they are able to do, to help them get things done.

Why are User-defined Functions So Important?

To keep it simple, a developer is going to have the option of either writing out some of their own functions, known as a **user-defined function**, or they are able to go through and borrow a function from another library, one that may not be directly associated with Python. These functions are sometimes going to provide us with a few advantages, depending on how and when we would like to use them in the code. Some of the things that we need to remember when working on these user-defined functions, to gain a better understanding of how they work, will include:

These functions are going to be made out of code blocks that are reusable. It is necessary to only write them out once. Then you can use them as many times as you need in the code. You can even take use user-defined functions in some of your other applications as well.

These functions can also be very useful. You can use them to help with anything that you want—from writing out specific logic in business to working on common utilities. You can also modify them based on your own requirements, to make the program work properly.

The code is often going to be friendly for developers, easy to maintain, and well-organized. This means that you are able to support the approach for modular design.

You are able to write out these types of functions independently. Also, the tasks of your project can be distributed for rapid application development, if needed.

A user-defined function that is thoughtfully well-defined can help ease the process for the development of an application.

Now that we know a little bit more about the basics of a user-defined function, it is time to look at some of the different arguments that can come with these functions, before moving on to some of the codes that you can use with this kind of function.

Options for Function Arguments

Any time that you are ready to work with these kinds of functions in your code, you will find that they have the ability to work with four types of arguments. These arguments and the meanings behind them will be pre-defined, and the developer is not always going to be able to change them up. Instead, the developer is going to have the option to use them, but also follow the rules that are there with them. You do get the option to add a bit to the rules to make the functions work the way that you want. As we said before, there are four argument types you can work with and these include:

- <u>Default Arguments:</u> In Python, we are going to find that there is a different way to represent the default values and the syntax for the arguments of your functions. These default values are going to indicate that the argument of the function is going to take that value, if you do not have a value for the argument which can pass through the call of the function. The best way to figure out where the default value will be is to look for the equal sign.

- <u>Required Argument:</u> These are the kinds of arguments that will be mandatory to the function that you are working on. These values need to go through and be passed in the right order and number, either when the function is called out or when the code will not be able to run the right way.

- <u>Keyword Arguments:</u> These are going to be the argument that will be able to help with the function call inside Python. These keywords are going to be the ones that we mention through the function call, along with some of the values that will go through this one. These keywords will be mapped with the function argument, so that you are able to identify all of the values, even if you do not keep the order the same when the code is called.

- <u>Variable Arguments:</u> The last argument that we are going to take a look at here is the variable number of arguments. This is a good one to work with when you are not sure how many arguments are going to be necessary for the code that you are writing, to pass the function. Otherwise, you can use this to design your code where any number of arguments can be passed, as long as they have been able to pass any requirements in the code that you set.

Writing a Function

Now that we have a little better idea of what these functions are like, and some of the argument types that are available in Python, it is time for us to learn the steps that you need to accomplish all of this. There are going to be four basic steps that we are able to use to make all of this happen, and it is really up to the programmer of how difficult or simple you would like this to be. We will start out with some of the basics, and then you can go through and make some adjustments as needed. Some of the steps that we need to take in order to write out our own user-defined functions are given below.

- Declare your function. You will need to use the 'def' keyword, and then have the name of the function come right after it.

- Write out the arguments. These need to be inside the two parentheses of the function. End this declaration with a colon, to keep up with the proper writing protocol in this language.

- Add in the statements that the program is supposed to execute at this time.

- End the function. You can choose whether you would like to do it with a return statement.

An example of the syntax that you would use when you want to make one of your own user-defined functions is:

def userDefFunction (arg1, arg2, arg3, ...):

program statement1

program statement2

program statement3

....

Return;

Working with functions can be a great way to ensure that your code is going to behave the way that you would like it to. Making sure that you get it set up in the proper manner can be really important as well. There are many times when the functions will come out and serve some purpose, so taking the time now to learn how to use them can be very important to the success of your code.

Python Modules

Modules consist of definitions as well as program statements.

An illustration is a file name **config.py** which is considered as a module. The module name would be **config.** Modules are used to help break large programs into smaller, manageable, and organized files, as well as promoting reusability of code.

Example

Creating the First module

Start IDLE.

Navigate to the **File** menu and click **New Window**.

Type the following:

Def add(x, y):   (This is a program to add two numbers and return the outcome)

Outcome: x+y

Return outcome

Import Module

The keyword import is used to import.

Example

Import first

The dot operator can help us access a function as long as we know the name of the module.

Example

Start IDLE.

Navigate to the **File** menu and click **New Window**.

Type the following:

first.add(6,8)

Import statement in Python

The import statement can be used to access the definitions within a module via the dot operator.

Start IDLE.

Navigate to the **File** menu and click **New Window**.

Type the following:

import math

print("The PI value is", math.pi)

Import with renaming

<u>Example</u>

Start IDLE.

Navigate to the **File** menu and click **New Window**.

Type the following:

import math as h

print("The PI value is-",h.pi)

In this case, h is our renamed math module with that saves typing time in some instances. When we rename, the new name becomes the valid and recognized one instead of the original one.

From…import statement Python.

It is possible to import particular names from a module, rather than importing the entire module.

Example

Start IDLE.

Navigate to the **File** menu and click **New Window**.

Type the following:

from math import pi

print("The PI value is-", pi)

Importing all names

Example

Start IDLE.

Navigate to the **File** menu and click **New Window**.

Type the following:

from math import*

print("The PI value is-", pi)

In this context, we are importing all definitions from a particular module. However, it is an encouraged norm as it can lead to unseen duplicates.

Module Search Path in Python

Example

Start IDLE.

Navigate to the **File** menu and click **New Window**.

Type the following:

import sys

sys.path

Python searches everywhere including the .sys file.

Reloading a Module

Python will only import a module once increasing efficiency in execution.

print("This program was executed") import mine

Reloading Code

Example

Start IDLE.

Navigate to the **File** menu and click **New Window**.

Type the following:

import mine

import mine

import mine

mine.reload(mine)

Dir() built-in Python function

For discovering names contained in a module, we use the **dir()** inbuilt function.

Syntax

dir(module_name)

Python Package

Files in Python hold modules, and directories are stored in packages. A single package in Python holds similar modules. Therefore, different modules should be placed in different Python packages.

CHAPTER 16:

Python Libraries

Python is distributed via a large library of modules that you can take advantage of. As a matter of fact, I suggest looking at what the Python standard library has to offer, before writing any of your own codes. For example, if you want to read and write CSV (comma-separated values) files, do not waste your time reinventing the wheel. Simply use Python's csv module. Do you want to enable logging in your program? Use the logging module. Do you want to make an HTTP request to a web service, and then parse the JSON response? Use the urllib.request and json modules. The list of what is available in the Python Standard Library is located here.

Let us use the **exit()** method from the sys module to cleanly terminate a program, if we encounter an error. In the following example, the **test.txt** file is opened. If the program encounters an error opening the file, the code block following **except:** will execute. If the reading of **test.txt** file is required for the remaining program to function correctly, there is no need to continue. The **exit()** method can take an exit code as an argument. If no exit code is provided, zero is used. By convention, when an error causes a program to exit, a non-zero exit code is expected.

import sys file_name = 'test.txt'

try: with open(file_name) as test_file: for line in test_file: print(line) except: print('Could not open {}.'.format(file_name)) sys.exit(1)

CHAPTER 17:

Object Oriented Programming

Object-oriented programming (OOP) is a programming paradigm in which programs are modeled according to their properties and behaviors rather than functions and logic. All these elements are then bundled into objects. Let us say, for example, an object could be you or me in real life. It could be a person with a valid name, age, birth date, occupation, and other data, called **properties** in terms of programming language.

Also, we have certain **behaviors**. We can walk, talk, work, sleep, jog, and others as well. So, OOP allows us to program and model real-world elements, and make them as realistic and meaningful as possible. Each entity in the world can be modeled as a Python object, which possesses some data and performs some function (has some behavior). What have we been doing till now? That is the procedural programming paradigm. It provides steps, functions, and code blocks that follow a sequential order of completing commands.

Let us take a look at the most basic concepts of OOP: the **classes**.

Classes and Objects

To model real-world objects in programming, we need a blueprint/ prototype of these objects on which these will be based on.

Classes are basically user-defined blueprints that state how an object should look, what attributes or properties its object should have, and what it should do (the behaviors).

Basically, we describe the general behavior of each object a class can have.

What are objects? **Objects** are instances of a class, that we work with, in life and programs.

This process, making objects from classes, is called **instantiation**.

Let us look at an example.

A car has the following attributes: color, number of tires, a model of the car, engine specifications, etc. When we program our class called 'Car,' these will act as the properties of our car.

Now, what does the car do? It drives, honks, and performs other functions internally. These are the properties or methods of our class 'Car.'

Every car performs these actions and has these properties; hence, classes are general representations of real-world objects.

Objects are the specific instances of these classes, and have relevant data in them. For example, a Ford Mustang will be different from an SUV, and have massively different properties.

Both of them are individual objects from our class 'Car.'

Writing Classes

Let us head back to our editor, and code an example class, with properties and behaviors.

Here is the code: (do not stress, I will explain everything later)

class Car:

'Modelling a car'

def __init__(self, model, license):

'Initialize all attributes and properties'

self.model = model

self.license = license

def drive(self):

print("Vroom vroom! The car drives!")

def honk(self):

print("HONK! HONK!")

fordMustang = Car("ford-8", "AX-2939")

SUV = Car("Honda", "MX-2101")

Now, onto the analysis of the code we just wrote.

An Explanation on Classes (Code Breakdown)

We begin by defining our class on line 1 using the 'class' keyword, and immediately following it is the name of the class.

Conventionally, we start the name of the class in uppercase letters.

In line 2, we define a **docstring**. It is a simple statement that tells us more about what the class has to offer, or what it does.

In line 4, we finally define a function, since we know that functions are defined using the 'def' keyword.

All functions defined in a class are called **methods** of that class.

The '__init__' is a special method provided by Python for every class, upon which the instantiation process runs automatically (when you create a new object).

A question you might have is why the underscores? They help you understand that it is a default function provided by Python, and it should not conflict with your own special function names.

Now, it takes in three parameters in our case, but it can have as many parameters as you want.

The self parameter is necessary and should come before others. What is self? The 'self' keyword is a reference that helps objects refer to themselves anywhere in the class.

It allows objects to have individual access to all the properties and methods defined in the class, and does not interfere with other objects.

The 'self' keyword is automatically passed whenever an object is made, and all other parameters can be passed with it (it is optional, but if used in the class declaration, they must be provided).

Now, in line 6, we prefix each parameter with self. This is so, each object of the class has its own specific attributes, and can be used throughout the class for that object only.

Next, we define two other functions and pass the 'self' parameter to it, which is necessary so each object has access to its own methods.

This is it for our class; let us see what happens next.

Making an Instance: Objects

Out of the scope of the class, we are finally using our class to make objects from it (or cars out of the class 'Car').

These are basically instructions for how our class should behave for a specific car.

We can make an object using this syntax:

objectOfTheClass = nameOfClass('param1', 'param2', ...)

Let us see how we did it for our example:

fordMustang = Car("ford-8", "AX-2939")

SUV = Car("Honda", "MX-2101")

Simply, we ask Python to make a car whose model is something, and the license is something else.

Again, we ask Python to make a different car with different data.

How Does It Work?

As soon as you instantiate an object and assign it, the interpreter runs the 'init' function, and assigns 'self' to the newly made object; it also associates the arguments that are passed to the parameters.

The 'init' method then returns an object, and it is assigned to our variable 'Ford Mustang.'

Now, let us use this object to see what attributes or properties our objects have.

Accessing Attributes and Methods

Try running the following code after instantiating your class:

print(fordMustang.model)

print(fordMustang.license)

It prints what we sent to it, using the arguments in our class.

As they are associated with our object now, the 'self' model is used to send back the data to us.

Here is the output:

```
ford-8
AX-2939
```

If you ask for these attributes from the second object, the output will be what you sent with it.

Here is an example:

print(SUV.model)

print(SUV.license)

```
Honda
MX-2101
```

Now, if you want to access the methods, simply use the dot operator again, and ask for the methods.

Here is how:

print(fordMustang.honk())

Outputs

```
HONK! HONK!
None
```

'None' is actually the return statement which is executed and printed.

Let us write a new method, and use an attribute to see different outputs for different objects (Add to your class from the last example):

def mileage(self):

val = input("What is the mileage? ")

print(self.model + " Mileage: " + val)

When you run this on a class, you will be prompted to enter a value, since we use the input() function. Enter the value and let us check the output:

```
What is the mileage? 2200
ford-8 Mileage: 2200
None
```

print(fordMustang.mileage())

Similarly, you can run this in the second class.

Inheritance

In real-world situations, most objects have a relationship to other objects.

Similarly, if we program something which is a specialized version of a more general element, this programming concept is called **inheritance,** where a child class grabs all properties and methods from the parent class, and makes use of them and adds something of its own. The parent class is the class, which is more general, and has all the basic functions. For example, if we wrote the code for a car, it is pretty general.

If now, we wish to write a class for an electric car, it will inherit most of the properties and behaviors from the parent class ('Car'), and add more stuff of its own.

Let us take a look at child classes next.

Child Classes: Writing One

We will model an electric car, a more specific form of our 'Car' class.

Here is the code and let us analyze it afterwards:

```python
class Car:
    def __init__(self, model, license):
        self.model = model
        self.license = license
    def drive(self):
        print("Vroom vroom! The car drives!")
    def mileage(self):
        val = input("What is the mileage? ")
        print(self.model + " Mileage: " + val)

class ElectricCar(Car):
    def __init__(self, model, license):
        super().__init__(model, license)

teslaX = ElectricCar("Tesla", "AA-9323")
print(teslaX.mileage())
print(teslaX.model)
```

```
What is the mileage? 343
Tesla Mileage: 343
None
Tesla
```

Firstly, we write our child class, and use the parenthesis to provide to it the parent class ('Car').

Next, we declare the 'init' function, just like we did before, and pass to it the parameters and the 'self' keyword, to refer to the object.

Next is something strange. We use the **super()** function and use the 'init' method, to refer to the 'init' method of the parent class.

This is done so a connection can be made between the parent class and the child class, and now, it can access all attributes and methods of the parent class.

Although it does not have any function of its own right now, it can definitely be added in later.

Next, we make an object of our an 'Electric Car' class, and ask for the methods and attributes which yield expected output, since now a relationship is made between the parent and child, i.e. **super** and **subclass**.

If you decide to assign methods to the child class, remember, the parent class cannot access them.

But, the child class can definitely (always) access the methods of the parent class.

Importing Classes

As your programs grow, so will the complexity, both in logic and file size.

It is always recommended to ship your classes as individual files, and import them wherever they are required.

This is possible using the import statements we studied a while ago.

Here is how you can import the classes into another file, and use them properly:

from car import Car

from car import ElectricCar

from car import Car, ElectricCar

from car import *

import car

CHAPTER 18:

Data Analysis

Python works great with data analysis, so let us look at what data analysis is all about and how we can use it for some of our own needs.

To start, data analysis is the process of cleaning, inspecting, transforming, and modeling our data. The objective is finding useful information in it, coming to sound conclusions, and supporting the decision making process of a company. This sounds like a lot for one process to handle, but when we use the right algorithms (supplied to us, and run by Python), it is definitely possible.

There are going to be a lot of different approaches and facets that come with our data analysis. When we put it all together, we can choose from a wide number of techniques to get it done. Often it depends on which method we like the most, and what information we are hoping to get out of the process as well. If our goal is to learn about our customers and how they behave, the data analysis we will completely different from if we are trying to learn more about the competition in our industry, or if we want to use it to make good business decisions.

When we use data analysis in statistics, we are able to divide it quite a bit. We can divide this into things like **exploratory data analysis**, **descriptive statistics**, and **confirmatory data analysis**. All of these are going to be important when it comes to our data analysis, and can move us forward to finding all of the insights and more, from the work that we do.

Another important aspect that we have to pay attention to, in our data analysis, is the fact that data has to be cleaned. **Data cleaning** is going to be a long process, but it allows us to correct all of the outliers that could mess with our results, and helps us to get rid of the other information that is unwanted and incorrect in the process. There are a number of these cleaning processes on the data, the use of which depend on the kind of data that we would like to clean. If you are working with things like quantitative data, then we can work with outlier detection, to help ensure that the anomalies in our data are taken care of. Even things like spellcheckers can be useful in case we are working with textual data, and need to deal with some of the words that have been mistyped.

In some cases, our data analysis is going to turn into a form of **business intelligence**. This is when the data analysis that we use runs heavily on aggregation, disaggregation, dicing and slicing, and even focusing on some of the information that is the most important to our business. This is just one of the forms that we are able to use, though. We can move into the world of **predictive analytics** as well, because this helps us to apply the statistical and the structural models that we have for some predictive forecasting when necessary. Alternatively, there is **text analytics** available, which is the application of the statistical, structural, and linguistic models to help us extract and classify the information that is found in the text.

While all of these forms handle data in a slightly different manner, and we are going to use them in a manner that is different from one another, they are all important and we need to spend time on them. In addition, all of them, even though they may seem to be completely different from one another, are going to be types of data analysis!

Many businesses want to jump on board with this kind of analysis. They have heard about the great results that many other companies have experienced with this, and they want to be able to achieve that as well. This makes it the perfect choice for them to at least look into, and you will find, with a bit of research, that almost any industry is able to benefit when they start to complete their own data analysis.

This is already such a big part of our world. Companies in all of the different industries are finding that this is the way of the future. It helps them make better products that customers want, make better decisions, beat out the competition, and even helps them to reach their customers in new and innovative manners. Because of all the benefits that come with the data analysis, it is no wonder that so many businesses are interested in data analysis, and are making sure that they can use it in the proper manner.

When it comes to working with data analysis, there are going to be a few phases that you will work in. These phases will ensure that you can handle the data in the proper manner, and that it will work the way that we want it to. These include some of the initial phases of cleaning our data, finding whether the data is of high enough quality, performing quality measurement analysis, and then entering main data analysis.

All of these steps are going to be important in data analysis. Even though some steps may seem to have nothing to do with data analysis in the first place, without all of them, our analysis is not going to be very accurate or good. Since companies are often going to rely on these analyses for important decisions, having accurate and high-quality data is going to be important.

The first step that we need to focus on here is **data cleaning**. This is the first process, and while it may not be as much fun as we see with the algorithms and more that come with data analysis, they are still important. This is where we match up records, check for multiples and duplicates in the data, and get rid of anything that is false or that does not match with what we are looking for.

When that part is done, it is time for us to do a bit of quality assurance here. We want to make sure that the data we work with is going to work for any algorithm that we would like to focus our time and attention on. Using things like frequency counts and descriptive statistics can help us out in this.

It is never a good idea to go through and analyze data that does not meet some of your own personal standards. You want to make sure that it will match with what you want to do with some of your work on the analysis. Ensure that it is accurate, and it will get the job done for you, as well.

When the **quality analysis** part is done, it is time to make sure that the measurement tools that we use here are going to be high in quality as well. If you are not using the same measurements on each part of this, then your results will be skewed in the process. If you are using the right ones, you will find that this gives you some options that are more accurate, and can help you really rely on the data analysis.

Once the cleaning the data, quality analysis and the measurement is done, it is time to dive into the analysis that we want to do. There are many different analysis that we can do on the information, and it often will depend on what your goals are in this whole process. We can go through and do some graphical techniques that include scattering plots. We can work with some frequency counts, to see what percentages and numbers are present. We can do some continuous variables or even the computation of new variables.

There are tons of algorithms that are present when we work on this, and it will again depend on your goals. Some are better for helping you see the best decision and make out of several options, such as the *decision tree* and *random forest*. Others are going to be better for helping us to sort through our information and see what patterns there are, such as the *clustering algorithms*. Having a good idea of what you are looking for out of the data, and what you hope to gain from it can make a world of difference.

Why Choose Python for Data Analysis?

At some point in your data analysis, you will need to create models or algorithms that will allow you to sort through that data, and find the insights that work the best for you. This is hard to do sometimes, and some challenging codes will come with it. However, as we will discuss in this chapter, the Python language can make it as simple to work with.

It is Easy to Read and Simple
We are going to start this off by looking at some of the reasons why Python, in particular, is such a good coding language to choose for our data analysis needs. There are other languages that we can work with, and they do a very good job as well. However, there are some wonderful things about Python that

help to push it above the rest, and which will ensure that you will get the best results when you work on this process as well.

The Libraries are Nice to Work with

As is the case when we look at some of the other popular coding languages, the libraries that come with Python will really lead to the success that you can see. In fact, right now, it is believed that in the Python Package Index, there are about 72,000 libraries, and this number is constantly growing.

Now, those are just two of the different libraries that we can focus on when we go through this process. If you want to know about a few more of the options, or you need something that is a bit more specialized, you will still be able to find it. Some of the other choices that a programmer can make when they work with data analysis and the Python language include:

- SciPy: This is going to be similar to NumPy, but it focuses more on the sciences that we need. It is also good at providing us with some tools and techniques, so that we can analyze the scientific data to meet our needs.

- Statsmodels: This library is going to focus more on some of the tools that are used for statistical analysis.

- Scikit-Learn and PyBrain: These two libraries are going to be focused more on machine learning. They are good ones to use when you need some modules for building neural networks and doing some data pre-processing.

- SymPy: This is going to be a good one to use for statistical applications.

- PyMC PyLearn2, Shogun: This is a good one to help with machine learning work.

- Matplotlib, Seaborn, and Plotly: As we will discuss as we go through this guide, the visuals that come with your analysis are going to be important. The three libraries, that we have above, are going to be good ones to help you turn your data into a visual, to help you see what insights and patterns there are, a little bit better.

Remember that these are just a few of the libraries that you can work within data analysis. There are libraries, and most of them are free to use, which are available for pretty much anything you want to do in the Python and data analysis world. Moreover, this is one of the benefits of working with Python here. It allows us to come out and work with any library and extension that we want. In addition, if there happens not to be an available library to work with, then there is the option, since Python is open-sourced, for us to go out there and make one of our own to meet this need.

CHAPTER 19:

Machine Learning

What is Machine Learning?

With the changing face of technology, machines with artificial intelligence have become responsible for tasks such as prediction, diagnosis, recognition, etc. These types of machines 'learn' from data that is added to them. This data is called training data because it is used to train the machine. The machines analyze patterns in this data and then put these patterns to use. Machines use different learning mechanisms to analyze the data depending on the actions they are required to perform, and they can be divided into two categories—unsupervised learning and supervised learning.

People may wonder why machines are not designed specifically for the tasks that they need to carry out, but there are many reasons as to why machine learning is advantageous. As mentioned earlier, research into the field of machine learning can help us better understand certain aspects of human learning, and machine learning can increase the accuracy and efficiency of machines.

Machine learning is also intertwined with the field of data mining. **Data mining** is essentially the process of looking through vast amounts of data to find important correlations and relationships. This is another advantage of machine learning as it might lead to the finding of important information.

On many occasions, humans design machines without correctly estimating the surrounding conditions in which they will be functioning, which can play a huge role in the performance of the machine. In such cases, machine learning can help in the acclimation of the machine to its environment, in order for the performance to not be hindered. In addition, environmental changes may occur, and machine learning will help the machine to adapt to these changes without missing performance.

Another loophole in the hard coding process from human beings into the machine is the fact that the process might be extremely elaborate. In such a case, the programmer might miss a few details, since it would be a very tedious job to encode all the details. Therefore, it is much more desirable to allow the machine to learn such processes.

There are constant changes in the world; in technology, vocabulary, and in many other areas. Redesigning systems to accommodate every change is impractical. Instead, machine-learning methods can be used to train the machines to adapt to these changes.

Advantages of Machine Learning

Now that we understand what machine learning is, given below are a few advantages.

One can use machine learning to handle multi-variety and multidimensional data in static and dynamic environments.

Machine learning helps to improve the efficiency of processes, thereby improving an individual's productivity.

You can use different machine learning tools to provide high-quality work, regardless of the complexity of the process.

There are many practical advantages for machine learning. For instance, you can develop autonomous software programs and computers. This helps to automate some tasks.

Disadvantages of Machine Learning

One of the major problems with machine learning is the acquisition. Since the data uses different algorithms, it will first need to be processed, to ensure that the algorithm produces the desired results.

Since some machine learning algorithms have to interpret the input, the developer must find a way to determine the effectiveness of the algorithm that is sometimes difficult to do.

The uses of machine learning algorithms are limited, and you can never be certain that an algorithm will work in every case you can think of. Therefore, before you use or apply a machine-learning algorithm, you must fully understand it, and verify that it will work for your problem.

Machine learning algorithms, like deep learning algorithms, must be trained using a training dataset. In most cases, you have a large dataset, which is difficult to work with.

It is also important to note that machine-learning algorithms are susceptible to errors. If the algorithm does make an error, it becomes difficult to diagnose and correct that error, since you will need to go through the underlying complexities of the algorithm. A machine-learning algorithm does not always make a prediction immediately. You should also remember that the algorithm learns through historical data; therefore, this algorithm is not always exposed to the ongoing situation. This deteriorates the performance of the algorithm.

Applications of Machine Learning

Today, machine learning is transforming the way businesses are run, by operating on the vast data that is now available, and drawing meaningful information and predictions from it.

Machine learning is now a solution to tasks that would be impossible to complete manually in such a short time, and with such a large amount of data. In this decade, we are bombarded with data and information and have no manual way of processing this information, thus paving the way for automated processes and machines to do that job for us.

Useful information can be derived when the process of analysis and discovery becomes automated, which will help us drive our future actions in an automated process. We have therefore entered the world of business analytics, data science, and big data. Business intelligence and predictive analytics are no longer just for the elite, as they are now accessible to small companies and businesses. This has given these small businesses a chance to participate in the process of collecting and utilizing information effectively. Let us look at some technical uses of machine learning, and how they can be applied to real-world problems.

Density Estimation

This use of machine learning allows the system to use the data provided to create a product that looks like it. For instance, if you were to pick up *War and Peace* from the shelves of a bookstore and run it through a machine, the machine would be able to determine the density of the words in the book, and provide us with similar novels.

Latent Variables

When you work with latent variables, the machine uses the method of clustering to determine whether the variables are related to one another. This is a useful tool when you do not know what the cause of change in different variables is, and when you do not know the relationship between these variables. Additionally, when the data set is large, it is better to look for latent variables as it helps to comprehend the data obtained.

Reduction of Dimensionality

Most of the time, the data obtained have different variables and dimensions. If there are more than three dimensions, it is impossible for the human mind to visualize the data. In these instances, machine learning can help in reducing the data into a manageable number of dimensions, so that the user easily understands the relationship between the different variables.

Visualization

Sometimes, the user would just like to visualize the existing relationship between variables or would like to obtain a data summary in visual form. In these instances, machine learning helps by summarizing the data for the user, using specified or non-specified parameters.

To summarize the main points, machine learning models train systems to learn from existing data, and offer various services such as prediction and classification which have several real-life applications, such as self-driving cars, phones with face recognition, or devices such as Google Home and Alexa, which respond to your accent with more accuracy the longer you use it.

Today machine learning and artificial intelligence are revamping the way healthcare institutions, publishing companies, weather predictors, travel fare and route predictors, and several other traditional domains are run. For example, in healthcare, machine learning is assisting in every phase, from predicting the potential health risks based on family history, to a full diagnosis of ailments.

Other everyday examples of machine learning include predicting stock market prices, platforms such as YouTube or Netflix recommending content based on your history, and Gmail detecting and classifying emails into the spam folder.

CHAPTER 20:

Network Security with Python.

Components of a Neural Network

Neural networks are going to be one of the frameworks that you can implement in machine learning. They try to mimic the way that the natural biological neural networks in humans operate.

The human mind is pretty amazing. It is able to look at a lot of different things around us, and identify patterns with a very high degree of accuracy. Any time that you go on a drive and see a cow, for example, you will recognize it at a cow. This applies to any other things that you are going to see when you are out on the road. The reason that we are able to do this is that we have learned over a period of time how these items look, and what can differentiate one item from another.

The goal of an artificial neural network is to be able to mimic, as closely as possible, the way that the human brain works. A complex architecture can make this happen. When it is in place, it allows the system to do a lot of amazing things that it would not be able to do in other situations. Let us take a look at how these neural networks can work, and why they are so amazing for our work with machine learning.

A neuron makes up the body of a cell, with a few extensions coming from it. The majority of these extensions are going to be in the form of a branch that is known as a dendrite. A long process, or a branching, exists, and this part is known as the axon. The transmission of signals begins at a region in this axon, and that is known as the hillock.

The neuron has a boundary that we call the cell membrane. A potential difference exists between the outside and the inside of this cell membrane, and that difference is called the membrane. If you are able to get the input to be big enough, then some action potential is going to be generated. This action potential will then travel all the way down the axon, and head away from the body of the cell.

A neuron is going to come next. This neuron is connected up with another neuron, and down the line with the help of a synapse. The information is going to head out of the neuron through the axon, and then it is passed on to the synapses and to the neuron, which is going to receive the message. Note that the neuron is only going to fire once the threshold has gone above the amount that is specified. The signals in this process are going to be important, because they are going to be received by the other neurons in the chain. The neurons are going to use signals to help them communicate with one another.

When it comes to the synapses, they can either be excitatory or inhibitory. When a spike or a signal arrives in one of the excitatory synapses, the receiving neuron is going to be caught on fire. If the signals are going to be inhibitory, then the neuron is not going to be fired onward.

The synapses and the cell body are going to be able to work together to calculate the differences that are there between the excitatory inputs and the inhibitory inputs. If there is a big difference here, then the neurons are told to fire the message down the line.

These types of networks are going to be used a lot, because they are great at learning and analyzing patterns, by looking at it in several different layers. Each layer that it goes through will spend its time seeing if there is a pattern that is inside the image. If the neural network does find a new pattern, it is going to activate the process to help the next layer start. This process will continue going on and on, until all the layers in that algorithm are created and the program is able to predict what is in the image.

Now, there are going to be several things that are going to happen from this point on. If the algorithm went through all the layers, and then was able to use that information to make an accurate prediction, the neurons are going to become stronger. This result is a good association between the patterns and the objects, and the system will be more efficient at doing this the next time you use the program.

This may seem a bit complicated, so let us take a look at how these neural networks will work together. Let us say that you are trying to create a program that can take the input of a picture, and then recognize that there is a car in that picture. It will be able to do this based on the features that are in the car, including the color of the car, the number on the license plate, etc.

When you are working with some of the conventional coding methods that are available, this process can be really difficult to do. You will find that the neural network system can make this a really easy system to work with.

For the algorithm to work, you would need to provide the system with an image of the car. The neural network would then be able to look over the picture. It would start with the first layer, which would be the outside edges of the car. Then it would go through a number of other layers, that help the neural network understand if there were any unique characteristics that are present in the picture, that outline that it is a car. If the program is good at the job, it is going to get better at finding the smallest details of the car, including things like its windows and even wheel patterns.

Now, when you are working on this, you may notice that there could potentially be a ton of layers that work with it. The more details and the more layers that you decide to find, the more accurate the prediction of the neural network is going to be. When there are more layers, there are more chances that the algorithm is going to be able to learn along the way. From then on, the algorithm is going to get better at making predictions, and will be able to do it with more accuracy, and faster, going forward.

This is a good algorithm to use when you want to have it recognize pictures, or even with some of the facial recognition software that is out there. With these, there is no possible way that you can input all of the possible information that is needed. So, working with the neural networks, where the program is able to learn things along the way, can really make a difference in whether the program is going to work or not.

Backpropagation

For you to work on training a neural network to do a certain task at the right time, the units of each part need to be adjusted. This ensures that there is a reduction in the amount of error that happens between the target output and the actual output. What this means is that the derivatives of the weights need to be computed by the network. So, this means that the network has to be able to monitor the changes in error, as the weights are decreased or increased based on the situation. The backpropagation algorithm is the one that you will choose to help you figure this part out.

If you plan on having the network units you work with becoming linear, then this is an easy enough algorithm to understand. With the linear options, the algorithm is going to be able to get the error derivative of the weights, by determining the rate at which the error is changing as the unit is activity level is being changed. When we are looking at the situation with the output units, the derivative of the error is going to be obtained when we can figure out the difference between the target output and the real output. To help us find any change rate in error for the hidden unit in a layer, all the weights between the hidden unit and the output unit, which it has been connected to, has to be determined ahead of time.

To help us with this part, we then need to go through and multiply the weights by error derivatives in the weights, and then the product that is added together. The answer that you are able to get here is going to be equal to the change rate in error for your hidden unit.

Once you have this error change rate, you can then go ahead and calculate the error change rate for all of the other layers that you want to work with. The calculation that you get for these is going to be done from one layer to the next, and in the opposite direction from where you would like the message to head through the network.

Profiting from Neural Networks

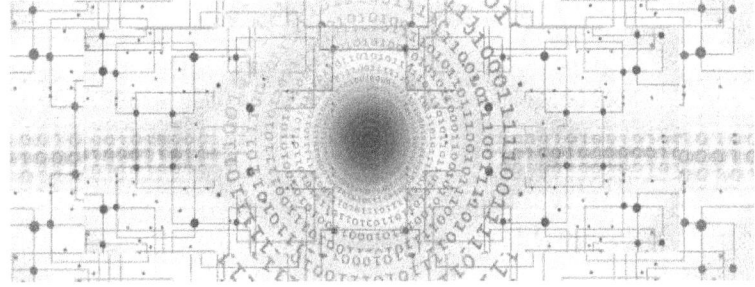

Neural networks are great if you want to be able to create different things that are automated within a computer or a process. They are even better, though, when you are able to take the time that you need and start to profit from them. Profiting from your neural networks is so much more than simply being able to add the different options to your computers. You can now use neural networks to be able to make huge profits within the stock markets, and even in forex markets.

Now that neural networks are becoming more popular, and they are able to be self-taught, you can use them for more things than what you were ever able to do in the past. Your neural networks need to be adjusted to be able to reach different levels, and you should make sure that you are going to be able to include all of the different money-making skills in, with the information you learn about them.

When you know how to make a neural network, you have more than just a skill – you have a profitable skill that you can use to build capital and create financial freedom for yourself.

Computers Over Brains

Human brains are great because they are intuitive but neural networks are able to become nearly as intuitive as the brain. When they are trained to be self-taught in the right way, they will be able to make the best decisions when it comes to the options that are included with neural networks.

In the past, humans were the preferred method that were traditionally used for trading. While some computers were able to help trade on an intuitive level, they were not able to pick up on the same things that humans could.

With neural networks, people do not really need to be involved in the trading process.

Specific Money-Making Definition

The ability of a neural network to make money is completely dependent on its ability to be able to learn the different things that the administrator has taught the network to be able to do. It is important to make sure that you are getting the best experience possible with your neural network, by including everything that you want it to do. If you set up your network to trade, and learn how to interact with the various aspects of the stimuli that are going into it with the trading sector, you will be able to make money from it.

Training Through Data

The best way to get your network to make money when you are doing different things with it is to push various types of data through it. This will allow the computer to 'learn' the data, and learn how to interact with it. It is a training process that the neural network needs to be able to go through in different areas that it is in. You should make sure that you are doing what you can to be able to get the neural network adjusted to your trading abilities.

Rules Created for Networks

When you are working with the neural network and you are pushing the data through, you will need to set up some rules at the beginning of the trading process. This will mean that you will need to pay close attention to the different things that it is doing, and the way that different types of stimuli are pushing through it. While you are watching it, you should change the rules that you set for your neural network.

Working Them for Monetary Gain

As you are learning more about neural networks and the different things that go on with it, you will learn the way that you can make money from them. Money can be made in many different ways through neural networks. The most popular ways are through creating them for other entities, and through trading with them. You can also invest in neural networks, but the return on that takes quite a long time, and is often not worth the time that you have to wait to see on it.

Trading System

There is an entire trading system that is associated with neural networks. People can buy, trade, sell, and move around the different networks that they have. The different entities that are a part of the neural network trading field will help to determine the amount that is included with the trading. When you are working in neural networks, it is worth looking into the trade field that comes along with it – some people will pay a lot of money for the creation of these networks, while others will pay to trade the different aspects of the network that they have created. While the trading plays a huge role in the buildup of capital with your neural network, it will also help to create a sense of community within the network.

Investing Through Networks

The investment that you make into a neural network while building it is usually your time. There are generally not very high costs that are associated with neural networks, but you should always be prepared for the costs that you might incur while you are using the neural network. You can, instead, invest in the actual neural network business. You can do this if you want to get returns on your trading, and if you are going to be able to increase the amount of money that you have for neural investing.

CHAPTER 21:

Web applications

A web application runs on a remote server as a software application. Most of the time, web browsers are for web applications like the internet. Some of the applications are used for intranets, schools, firms, and organizations. They are not the same as other applications, since you do not need to install them. Some of the common web applications include Flickr, Wikipedia, Facebook, and Mibbit. They are popular as most of the operating systems are on the web browser and programmers can change them with ease.

Several benefits come with using web application:

- They do not need to be installed since they run inside a browser.

- They do not require a lot of space for storage; only a display of data is needed.

- Web applications help with compatibility problems; all that is needed is a browser.

- Most of the data used is remotely stored; hence, ease of cooperation and communication.

- Web application helps in mail and communication.

Apart from the listed benefits of web applications, there are also drawbacks:

- Most of the known web applications seem to look different as compared to the regular programs. The reason is that they run inside a browser. The user experience might be different and not liked by many.

- To be able to follow standards, web applications need to be coded, and any small changes will prevent the web application to be used in any browser.

- There is a need to have a connection between the web application and the server in order for it to run smoothly. For the connection to happen, you will need bandwidth. When the connection is not adequate, you may experience data loss, or the application may be unstable.

- Most of the web applications depend on the server that hosts them. When it is off, the web application is not usable, but the traditional applications will still work.

- The overall control of the web application is with the mother company. They have the power to create a new version when they feel like it.

- When the data is remotely stored, exporting it to be used by other applications will be hard.

- Web applications enable the company to track all the activities of the users, hence privacy issues.

At this point, you need to know how a web application works. Most of the web applications are coded in a language that is browser supported, like HTML or JavaScript. The main reason is that the languages depend on the browser in order to execute their programs. You should know that some of these applications are dynamic, and they will require server-side processing. Others are considered static, and will not need any processing from the server.

When you have a web application, you will need a webserver to manage all the requests that the client has. The server will help in performing all the tasks, and store data and information. The application servers includes ASP, PHP, and JSP. A normal web application has a specific flow:

- The user will trigger a request using the internet that goes to the webserver. This can be done through the web browser or user interface on the application.

- The web server will then forward that request to the specific web application server.

- The requested task will be performed by the web application server; this includes querying the database and data processing, that will generate the required results.

- The results will be sent to the web server by the web application server; this is in regard to the data processed or the required information.

- The client will get a response from the web server; they will get the information that they have requested on the user's display.

- There are several examples of web applications such as shopping carts, word processors, online forms, file conversions, and scanning, online forms, and email programs like Yahoo and Gmail.

How to Work with Django

Django is used to create web applications. It is specifically meant to create a web application that connects to a database. You can also deal with user management, good security, and internationalization. Some of the common web applications include Disqus, Pinterest, and Instagram. You can use Django as standalone libraries, even though it will require extra work. That is the reason why it is not advisable to use it as a standalone tool.

Django is a combination of different components that work by responding to user requests.

The first step is having the request-or-response system. The main work is to receive and return web responses. Django will accept all the requests of the URLs and return all the HTML information to the web browser. The page can be in plain text or something better.

The web requests will enter the Django application through the URLs. The only entry point for any Django application is the URL; developers have the control over available URLs. When you access the URL, Django will enable the viewing.

All your requests will be processed by the views. Django views are considered to be codes generated from Python, when the URL is accessed. Views are something simple like returning a text to the user. The text can be made complex. It can be form processing, credit card processing, and database querying. When the view has completed processing, a web response is sent to the user.

When web response is returned, the user can access the URL on the browser they will access the response. This could be an HTML web page that shows a combination of images and text, and they are created using the templating system from Django.

With Django information, there is flexibility to have more applications. You can use that you create a simple blog, mobile applications, or a desktop. Django framework is powered by sites like Instagram and Pinterest.

User Accounts

A **user account** is on the network server that is used to store the username of the computer, password, and any relevant information. When you have the user account, it will allow you or not to connect with other computers or networks. With a network with multiple users, you will need user accounts. A good example of a user account is your email account.

There are different types of user accounts, regardless of the operating system that you are using. You will be able to trace, authenticate, and monitor all the services. When you install an operating system, it creates user accounts to have access after the installation. After the installation, you will have four user accounts: system account, super user account, regular and guest user account.

- **System account**: These are accounts that are used to access resources in the system. The operating system will use these accounts to know if a service is allowed to access the resources or not. When they are installed, they create relevant accounts. After installation, the account will be able to access the needed information. If you are a network or system administrator, you will not need to have any information about the accounts.

- **Super user account**: This account is privileged in the operating system. When one is using Windows, the account is referred to as the Administrator account. When using Linux, the account is the root account, and the operating system will help the user complete different tasks. Tasks are like starting services, creating and deleting new user accounts, installing new software, and changing system files.

- **Regular user account**: This account does not have many privileges and cannot make changes in the system properties and files. They only operate on tasks that they are authorized to, like running applications, creating files, and customizing variables.

- **The Guest user account**: This is the account that has less privilege; you will not be able to change anything with the system. The account is known to perform temporary tasks like playing games, watching movies, or browsing the internet. Using Windows, this account will be created after installation; in Linux, you will need to create the account manually after installation.

The next step is to know how to create a user account. When you have multiple users using the same computer, you will need to have new user accounts for each user. When using Windows, you can create several accounts. Each of the user accounts has its own settings. It will allow you to control the files separately, and when each user logs in, it will be like their own computer.

The first step in creating a user account is to click on **Start** on the **Control Panel** then click on **Add or Remove User Accounts**. Click on **Create a New Account** and choose the account type. You will enter the account name, and then select the account type that you wish to create. The administrator has the privilege to create and change accounts, and install programs. The difference is a standard user cannot perform such tasks. The last step will be to click on the **Create Account** button, and close the **Control Panel**.

How to Style and Deploy an App

There are different deployment options that need to be considered. When an app is developed in the application builder, it is created in the workplace. All the workplaces have IDs and names; all you need is to create an application in the development, and then deploy it in production.

During deployment, you will decide where you want the existing ID to be in the workplace; in the existing HTTP server, or in a new one. The deployment options are given below.

You will first create an application that is expressed by end-users. The best way to deploy an application is by creating an Application Express for end users. Then, send the URL and login details to the users. It will work when the user population is tolerant and small.

You will need to use the same schema and workplace. You need to export and then import the application, then install it under a different application ID. This strategy will work when there are fewer changes to any known objects.

Use the same schema and a different workplace; export all, and then import the applications into another workplace. It will prevent any production and modification by developers.

Use a different schema and workspace. Export and then import the application into a separate workplace, and install it in a separate schema.

Use a different database for all variations. Export, then import to another Oracle application, and then install it to a different database and schema.

To deploy an app, in the configuration manager console, click on **Software Library**. Go to **Application Management**, and then choose **Application** or **Application Group**.

Choose from an application or application group in the deploy list, and click **Deploy**.

CHAPTER 22:

Projects

Project 1

Solve these math equations written in Python syntax.

Exercise 1

(40**3) - 100

Exercise 2

(20/5) - (10/2)

Exercise 3

(2**3) - 2

Exercise 4

(6**1) - 1

Exercise 5

(5%2) + 1

Exercise 6

(2**4) + 5

Exercise 7

5 - (6%4)

Exercise 8

70 - (10**2)

Exercise 9

-6 - 2**2

Exercise 10

6 - (-1)

Exercise 11

Tell me what this program will print.

print #eat me

print "fear me"

var string = "eat me"

print string

Answers

Exercise 1. 63900

Exercise 2. -1

Exercise 3. 6

Exercise 4. 5

Exercise 5. 2

Exercise 6. 21

Exercise 7. 3

Exercise 8. -30

Exercise 9. -2

Exercise 10. 7

Exercise 11. This will print an error message because of the way the comment is placed on the first line.

Project 2

Here are some examples to work on.

Exercise 1. Create a program that solves this equation $x = 40(5) - 6^3$

Exercise 2. Create a program that prints out your favorite quote to the screen.

Exercise 3. Break up the quote from the above exercise, and store each word into a dictionary.

Exercise 4. Store those words in a tuple.

Exercise 5. Repeat Exercise 4 with an array.

Exercise 6. Create three variables with a floating point number, a string, and an integer. Print them to the screen.

Exercise 7. Create a multiple assignment with five variables and five different values. Print each value to the screen on individual lines.

Exercise 8. Create a variable, delete it, try to print it again. What happens after you print it again?

Exercise 9. Create a string with at least three words. Print the first character. Print the 2 through the 10 characters. Print the entire string starting from the third character.

Exercise 10. Make a list with at least two strings and two numbers. Print the first and third values on one line.

Answers

Keep in mind, these are just possible answers.

Exercise 1. The expression will look like (40*5) - (6**3). Bonus points if you had it print to the screen. :-)

Exercise 2. print "We the people."

Exercise 3. quote = {"word1": "We", "word2": "the", "word3": "people"}

Exercise 4. quote = ("We", "the", "people")

Exercise 5. quote = ["We", "the", "people"]

Exercise 6.

myStr = "Hello"

myFloat = 1.1

myNum = 10

print myStr

print myFloat

print myNum

This will print:

Hello

1.1

10

Exercise 7.

myVar1, myVar2, mVar3, myVar4, myVar5 = 1, "a", 2, "b", 3

print myVar1

print myVar2

print myVar3

print myVar4

print myVar5

This will print:

1

a

2

b

3

Exercise 8.

myVar = 1

del myVar

print myVar

You will get a null value.

Exercise 9

myString = "Hello, my name is John. How are you?"

print myString[0]

print myString[1:9]

print myString[2:]

Keep in mind, strings are zero-indexed just like arrays.

This will print

H

ello, my

llo, my name is John. How are you?

Exercise 10.

list = [1, "Hello", 2, "world]

print list[0],

print list[2]

This will print:

1 2

Conclusion

Programming is not just about getting a PC, to get things done. It is tied in with composing code that is helpful to people. Great programming is saddling complexity by composing code that rhymes with our instincts. Great code will be code that we can use with a negligible amount of setting, and right now, be gainful.

In conclusion, Python and big data provide one of the strongest capabilities in computational terms on the platform of big data analysis. If this is your first time at data programming, Python will be a much easier language to learn than any other, and will be far more user-friendly compared to other programming languages.

Python is a wonderful tool to use for data purposes, and I hope this guide stands you in good stead, as you go about using it for your purposes.

Python is a high-level language which is both interpreter based and object-oriented. This makes it easy for anybody to understand how the language works. You can also extend the programs that you build in Python onto other platforms. Most of the inbuilt libraries in Python offer a variety of functions, that make it easier to work with large data sets.

You will now have gathered that machine learning is a complex concept, but can easily be understood. You can now begin working on programming and building models in Python. Ensure that you diligently practice, since that is the only way you can improve your skills as a programmer.

At this point, you clearly understand who can use Python, and its importance to any economists and finance experts. The information will help to know how you can earn as a Python programmer, the basic concepts, and all the terms used in Python programming. You can now start your Python programming for data analysis, install Python, and visit the different places you can learn all this.

Regardless of what you expect to achieve with this knowledge, you have taken the first step in your quest to better understand neural networks and their role in our lives, today, tomorrow, and well on into the future.

There are a lot of other coding languages out there that you are able to work with, but Python is one of the best that works for most beginning programmers, as it provides the power and the ease of use that you are looking for when you first get started. This guidebook took the time to explore how Python works, along with some of the different types of coding that you can do with it.

www.ingramcontent.com/pod-product-compliance
Lightning Source LLC
Chambersburg PA
CBHW071354210526
45465CB00001B/86